LEARNING TO SHARE

VOLUME-THREE

All proceeds from the sale of the book go to INDRANI FOUNDATION (Registration No. 10385, Delhi) (working for social cause – supporting stray, wounded and sick animals and supporting educational activities of meritorious students from poor families).

Learning to Share Series

1. Learning to Share (Volume One): Experiences and Reflection on PRA and Community Participation/ **Neela Mukherjee, Vinita Kumar, Meera Jayaswal** and **Bratindi Jena** .
2. Learning to Share (Volume Two): Experiences and Reflections on PRA and other Participatory Approaches/ **Neela Mukherjee** and **Meera Jayaswal**

About the Author

Dr. Neela Mukherjee is currently working as a development practitioner, researcher, trainer and a resource person to multiple development organizations, both home and abroad. She is associated with "Development Tracks", an enterprise involved in cutting-edge research, training and consultancy activities. As a consultant to UNDP, IFAD, DFID, Asian Development Bank, World Bank, GEF and others, Dr. Mukherjee has worked in a host of developing countries. Formerly, a Professor of Economics at the LBS National Academy of Administration, Mussoorie, India and an alumna of the London School of Economics and Political Science, London, Dr. Mukherjee was also a senior consultant to ICRIER, New Delhi.

Dr. Rupa Dasgupta is a Scientist at the Regional Research Laboratory, Bhopal, a constituent R&D laboratory under the Council of Scientific & Industrial Research, New Delhi. Dr. Dasgupta is a Ph.D. in Physics with 16 years experience in R&D. Her R&D findings have been published in over 50 publications in international journals. Dr. Dasgupta was associated with the UNDP sub-programme under which participatory scientific research work with farmers in Madhya Pradesh was carried out in her capacity as a UNDP sub-programme manager.

LEARNING TO SHARE

Experiences and Reflections on Participatory Approaches

VOLUME-THREE

Edited by

NEELA MUKHERJEE
RUPA DASGUPTA

Published for

INDRANI FOUNDATION, NEW DELHI

by

CONCEPT PUBLISHING COMPANY, NEW DELHI-110059

Cataloging in Publication Data—DK

Courtesy: D.K. Agencies (P) Ltd. <docinfo@dkagencies.com>

Learning to share / edited by Neela Mukherjee ... [et al.]. v. cm.

Contributed articles.

Includes bibliographical references.

Includes index.

Contents: v. 1. Experiences and reflections on PRA and community participation—v. 2. Experiences and reflections on PRA and other participatory approaches—v. 3. Experiences and reflections on participatory approaches.

ISBN 8170226635 (set)

1. Participant observation. 2. Social participation —India. 3. Social action—India. 4. Community development—India. 5. Rural development—India.

I. Mukherjee, Neela.

DDC 302.140 954 21

ISBN 81-7022-663-5 (Series)
ISBN 81-8069-176-4 (Vol. 3)

First Published 2004

Published and Printed by
Ashok Kumar Mittal
Concept Publishing Company
A/15-16, Commercial Block, Mohan Garden
New Delhi-110059 (India)
Phones: 25351460, 25351794
Fax: 091-11-25357103
E-mail: publishing@conceptpub.com

EDITORIAL

The present edited volume is a collection of twelve papers, which is a sequel to Volumes One and Two of the series 'Learning to Share', published in 1997 and 2001 by the Concept Publishing Company. The first and second volume of 'Learning to Share' contributed towards documentation and sharing of PRA/PLA-type experience from the field. The present volume has been prepared with the same objective.

Similar to earlier volumes on "Learning to Share" this volume also assembles the experience of many authors. This volume hopes to carry forward the message of the "power of sharing" and people's participation to attain a wide variety of objectives ranging from needs assessment, community participation, enhancement of social capital, capacity building, resource mapping for planning, eliciting community worldviews, generating sustainable livelihood opportunities with policy implications.

Contributions to the book are from authors involved in participatory approaches from various backgrounds. There are some authors who have learnt from implementing participatory projects in the field while others have social development background and are pursuing participatory action research. In addition, scientists working with farmers have documented their experience in R&D and found the process useful for scientific research. Some students who are picking up participatory approaches have also produced field notes on the subject. The book has authors from varied background such as scientist, forester, social scientist, teacher, social worker, NGOs, administrators and students trying to learn from the grass roots.

The papers published in this book are mainly of two types—one type are those which are essentially topical with greater focus on applications of participatory approaches in the field while the other type has to do more with the emerging field methods in PRA/PLA. There are 12 papers/notes in this volume where 8 topical papers on participatory approaches include topics such as measuring social capital, livestock assessment, women's worldview on HIV-AIDS, institutional processes in watershed management, rural weavers' livelihoods, integrated human development, stakeholders' in Grameen bank (Bangladesh) and livelihood-based conservation (China). The papers based on methodological innovations are 4 in number, which include resource mapping, mobility in well-being, ownership/empowerment chappati and participatory technological package.

In her paper "Measuring Social Capital in Joint Forest Management", Neela Mukherjee discusses a framework for measurement of social capital at the local level and applies it in the context of 4 Forest Protection Committees (FPC's) under Joint Forest Management (JFM) at Midnapore, West Bengal. Field evidence from India and other countries shows that there is strong positive relationship between social capital and natural resource management/protection at the local level and appropriate ways of measuring social capital are important for assessing its progress. Based on three aspects of social capital, 'productivity', 'equity' and `sustainability', a range of criteria have been integrated in Mukherjee's framework for measurement of social capital. Criteria, such as group capacity and worldview, 'making sense' of JFM, internal norms, mutual trust, role clarity, equity in benefit-flows, livelihood impacts and ability to resolve conflicts have been considered as important for measuring social capital. Earlier version of the paper was published in the *Economic and Political Weekly*, July 20, 2002 and hosted in *www.livelihoods.org,* 2003.

In their paper "Participatory Appraisal for Improved Performance of Livestock", Mahesh Chander, Tanmay Samajdar and Sanjay Kumar bring in lessons from the field to explain how participatory approaches can improve the performance in the livestock sector, which is a vital sector for the Indian economy. The paper basically highlights the importance of livestock in Indian economy, role of PA methodologies in sustainable development, potential problems in PA application in the livestock sector and finally, the need for right kind of training for effective application of PA tools in the livestock sector for improved performance. In their paper the authors explain that a range of participatory tools can be effectively applied in research and development activities in the livestock sector. Since the field level experiences on the PAs concerning livestock development are still very limited, training at right places by the right people is essential for the effective use of PAs in the livestock sector. Finally, the authors recommend that the allocation for livestock research and development must significantly be increased so that the flow of funds for the PAs in different agro-climatic regions of the country could be jacked up.

The paper "Understanding HIV-AIDS: An Analysis of Women's Voices" by Meera Jayaswal, Kalindi Kumari, R.N. Bhagat and S.K. Sinha throws light on the awareness level of the women regarding AIDS. Based on a survey conducted by the authors amongst married women in the age group of 23 to 45 years the findings relate to (i) acquaintance with the disease, (ii) comparison of AIDS with other diseases, (iii) what happens to AIDS patients?, (iv) how AIDS happens?, (v) how AIDS can be prevented or treated, if possible and related issues.

Using participatory methods, the paper, shows that there is considerable ignorance, misconceptions and prejudice in relation to symptoms, cause and prevention of the disease. The paper concludes that in order to combat the AIDS threat, intervention is needed not only to enhance awareness level but also to change the prevailing prejudice against the disease. The recommendations of the authors include spreading awareness about the actual symptoms, prevention, and cure of the disease, and most importantly reducing/removing the attached social stigma with this difficult disease.

The paper "Enabling Processes in Doon Valley Watershed Management" by Jyotsna Sitling describes the process of the Doon Valley Watershed Management Project to eco-restore the Doon Valley. In the paper, the project activities in developing institutional, technical and financial infrastructure support have been explained and assessed. The paper describes how participation of the local communities has remained central to developing local capacity, initiative and institution for collective action. The paper also documents project processes based on cumulative learning and experience that have gradually enabled the hill communities to become independent of the project support. It also analyses the lessons learnt in adoption of participatory approaches by a Government agency in terms of sustainability of village institutions.

"The Story of Anandapur Weavers —A District Magistrate's Diary" by M.V. Rao documents the initial conditions of weavers' livelihoods and positive synergies created through interactive sessions with the weaver community in terms of learning their problems and issues and resolving them jointly step by step in partnership with the government. The paper shows how windows of opportunities were created through communication channels established between different stakeholders — weavers at the grassroots and the administration at the top.

The paper "Participation and Human Development: Bagdah Experience" by Hari Krishna Dwivedi and S.B. Roy is a description of the Bagdah experiment in North 24 Parganas in West Bengal, which aims to bring about improvement in the area of integrated development of health, education and resource management through community participation and savings on a sustained basis. The paper describes the mechanism of the experiment for community empowerment as well as women's empowerment. It also describes the ways for motivating and sensitising both the parties, viz., the members of the community organisation and the government staff.

The paper "Grameen Bank: Interactive Sessions with the Stakeholders" by Taponeel Mukherjee and Sourav Roy is based on interactive sessions with different stakeholders of the Grameen Bank in Sadipur, Bangladesh. The Grameen Bank model is well known and is being replicated in many countries across the world. The paper illuminates experience and views of different stakeholders—members of the bank and non-members about the effectiveness of Grameen Bank as a source of micro finance for its members and its role in alleviating poverty. Different case studies from Sadipur branch in Bangladesh presented by the paper show how productive activities through hard work and micro finance have helped the members step-by-step to come out of the poverty trap.

In her note "PRA in Livelihoods and Biodiversity Conservation: China", Neela Mukherjee describes exercises in PRA in 3 villages in a wetland of China and tries to draw policy implication based on the findings. The topic of biodiversity conservation in wetlands and sustainable livelihoods of local communities has attracted considerable attention in recent years. On the level of paradigm shift, local communities have been recognised as major stakeholders in wetland conservation. The present paper based on a case study from China draws lessons in biodiversity conservation in wetlands, eco-tourism and sustainability issues in local livelihoods.

The paper on "Participatory Resource Mapping of Villages" by Rupa Dasgupta, Swati Lahiri, R. Soni, Robi Dasgupta and M.V.R.L. Murthy describes a novel method of resource identification of villages through people's participation. The method relates to people's mapping the resources available in a village. The village map thus generated is extended to a number of villages, which are then consolidated to get a resource map of the entire block. A resource map thus developed can then be used for a number of purposes such as designing of infrastructure, planning for development, connectivity through roads etc., planning for industrial and entrepreneurial units, establishing markets, and similar activities.

In the paper "Upward-Downward Mobility in Well-Being" by Debabrata Basu, Durba Biswas and Rupak Goswami the wealth ranking method in PRA has been taken a step forward to measure the changes in well-being through the tool of upward-downward mobility. The paper discusses how the well-being of people often changes absolutely as well as relatively over time with or without interventions. Upward and downward mobility of the people along the well-being ladder helps to understand the impact of local realities and their interactions with the external factors of influence.

The paper "Participatory Area Selection for Technological Intervention" by Rupa Dasgupta, Swati Lahiri, A.K. Jha and M.V.R.L. Murthy centres around selecting and applying relevant technology in rural areas to improve economic conditions of the villagers for their benefit. Application of technology in rural areas should be based on people's needs and also based on raw materials available locally. The technology intended can be either resource based, skill based or pertaining to the service sector. The paper describes a methodology, which may be adopted, in selecting the required technological intervention from amongst the demands of the local people based on local raw material, skill, infrastructure and other local resources.

The note "Innovations from the Field: The Ownership/Empowerment Chappati" by Neela Mukherjee, Shaista Khan and Rekha Bahuguna makes the point that PRA methods are never static. They are flexible, innovative and adaptive to local situation. Their strength lies in ways that they can be moulded to suit local context, circumstances and issues. In recent years there has taken place innovation and adaptation in Chappati/institutional diagramming at the field level so as to tailor them to measure "ownership", "empowerment", "decision-making", "involvement", "relationship", "accountability", "participation" and other social aspects of institutional development. The note describes some innovative ways of doing Chappati diagramming based on field experience in India.

In this volume, we have tried to cover a range of experience, as shown above, both in terms of application of participatory approaches and evolution of field methods. There are many shortcomings of this book for we know how complex it is to capture 'field reality' through the writing process. However, it is important to document and share field experience as much as possible. And we would like to continue this series for future documentation of our experiences and lessons from the field.

Our thanks are to those who encouraged us to edit this series on "Learning To Share" and contributed papers for this volume. We express our sincere thanks to Ashok Mittal of the Concept Publishing Company who has taken a keen interest in the publication of this series.

The amount received as royalty from the publication of Volume One and Two "Learning To Share" was donated to Friendicoes, a Society in Delhi involved in eradication of cruelty to animals. This time the amount will be donated to Indrani Foundation to support similar activities.

The book is meant for all those who are interested and involved in the area of participatory development. We hope the readers find this book interesting and useful.

NEELA MUKHERJEE
and
RUPA DASGUPTA

2 February 2004

CONTENTS

ABBREVIATIONS

COREMA	–	Cluster of Resource Management Association
DM	–	District Magistrate
GAREMA	–	Village Resource Management Association
GOI	–	Government of India
PLA	–	Participatory Learning and Action
PRA	–	Participatory Rural Appraisal
PRI	–	Panchayati Raj Institutions
SHG	–	Self-Help Group
WMD–		Watershed Management Directorate

LIST OF TABLES

LIST OF CHARTS

LIST OF FIGURES

LIST OF CONTRIBUTORS

Dr. Neela Mukherjee is a development practitioner, researcher, trainer and a resource person associated with "Development Tracks", an enterprise involved in cutting-edge research, training and consultancy activities.

Dr. Mahesh Chander, a Senior Scientist (Extension Education) with Indian Council of Agricultural Research (ICAR) at Indian Veterinary Research Institute (IVRI), Izatnagar has been engaged for long years in research, teaching and field extension activities for participatory livestock development.

Tanmay Samajdar, a veterinary graduate is pursuing his doctoral studies at IVRI in the discipline of Veterinary Extension Education.

Dr. Sanjay Kumar is Senior Scale Scientist (Agricultural Economics) with ICAR and currently posted at Indian Veterinary Research Institute, Izatnagar.

Dr. Meera Jayaswal is associated with the PG Department of Psychology, Ranchi University, Ranchi.

Dr. Kalindi Kumari is associated with P.P.K. College, Bundu, Jharkhand.

Dr. R.N. Bhagat is a Senior Medical Officer, Kargali Central Hospital, Bokaro, Jharkhand.

Dr. S.K. Sinha is Head of the Post-Graduate Department of Psychology, Ranchi University, Ranchi.

Jyotsna Sitling, an officer of the Indian Forest Service is an experienced systems developer on community based natural resource management practices especially in relation to forests and sustainable livelihood processes.

M. V. Rao, an officer of the Indian Administrative Service is currently posted as District Magistrate, Paschim Medinipur district in West Bengal and involved in facilitating 27,000 Self Help Groups.

Hari Krishna Dwivedi, an officer of the Indian Administrative Service is currently posted as District Magistrate, 24-Parganas North district in West Bengal and involved in facilitating integrated development process.

Dr. S. B. Roy is the Chairman of IBRAD in Kolkata, a reputed NGO and has written and taught extensively on participatory natural resource management.

Taponeel Mukherjee is a student of Economics at Stony Brook University, New York. In 2002, he worked as an intern at the Grameen Bank, Bangladesh.

Sourav Roy is a student of Economics at Hans Raj College, Delhi University. In 2002, he worked as an intern at the Grameen Bank, Bangladesh.

Dr. Rupa Dasgupta is a Scientist at the Regional Research Laboratory, Bhopal.

Dr. Swati Lahiri is a Scientist at the Regional Research Laboratory, Bhopal.

Dr. R. Soni is a Scientist at the Regional Research Laboratory, Bhopal.

Dr. Robi Dasgupta is a Scientist at the Regional Research Laboratory, Bhopal.

Dr. A.K. Jha is a Scientist at the Regional Research Laboratory, Bhopal.

Dr. MVRL Murthy is a Scientist at the Regional Research Laboratory, Bhopal.

Dr. Debabrata Basu is a Reader in the Department of Agricultural Extension, Bidhan Chandra Krishi Viswavidyalaya, Mohanpur, Nadia, West Bengal.

Durba Biswas and **Rupak Goswami** are doctoral students in the Department of Agricultural Extension, Bidhan Chandra Krishi Viswavidyalaya, Mohanpur, Nadia, West Bengal.

Shaista Khan and **Rekha Bahuguna** were social mobilisers for the Doon Valley Watershed Project.

1

MEASURING SOCIAL CAPITAL IN JOINT FOREST MANAGEMENT

NEELA MUKHERJEE

In recent times 'social capital' has caught the attention of many development practitioners and academicians. Mutual trust and cooperation amongst members of communities is a significant factor explaining institutional performance (Putnam *et al.*, 1993). Drawing from Putnam *et al.*, (1993) the features of social organization that enhance trust and cooperation increase societies' well being by making institutions more democratic and efficient in delivering public goods and services. Field evidence points out that when active involvement is sought of local communities for organizing themselves based on their knowledge and experience in planning and implementation of projects, the higher becomes the possibility of sustaining development initiatives (Uphoff, 1992; Pretty, 1995; Pretty *et al.*, 2001; Cernea, 1991; Mukherjee,1997). Field results are indicative of the fact that social capital formation at the local level is crucial for natural resource management/protection.

In this context one oft-repeated question is why are some local level institutions relatively successful than others in managing localized natural resources. Do they have more social capital than others? What then are the reasonable constituents of social capital and how do they influence management of natural resources? The core issue in this context is how to measure social capital. Serra (2001) attempted measurement of social capital at the national level. The present analysis makes a rudimentary attempt to measure social capital in the context of localized management of natural resources. The paper adopts a qualitative framework for measurement and applies it in the context of four Forest Protection Committees (FPC) of Joint Forest Management (JFM) at Kalaikunda Range, in Midnapore, West Bengal. The qualitative scores are then quantified to arrive at aggregate scores on social capital for each FPC. For the sake of simplicity, all criteria in this exercise have been treated as having equal weights though in practice the weights tend to differ across criteria. Such measurement of social capital is important at the local level for reasons more than one. It provides an idea of the progress made by local institutions in terms of building social capital and how it relates to natural resource management. It can also be applied as a participatory monitoring tool for finding out areas of weaknesses and strengths and undertaking mid-way corrections, if any, for strengthening social capital.

A Framework for Measuring Social Capital

Three generic criteria have been considered for measuring social capital of institutions. These criteria are as follows.

- Productivity
- Equity
- Sustainability

Based on the three generic criteria as above, specific measures have been considered. The generic criterion for measuring 'productivity' includes those criteria, which enhance productivity or growth of social capital. Group membership is important because broader the membership-base more is the coverage of people coming together for a cause. The type of leadership determines the drive of the group. Keenness and sense of group responsibility are to the advantage of a group in achieving group objectives. With positive group interactions the capacity of the group improves over time and the confidence of group members go up with more experience. External linkages, both vertical and horizontal determine 'connectedness' of the group and provide opportunities for growth. Improved technologies lead to more efficiency in group-based activities.

The criteria related to 'productivity' are listed below.

Criteria for Productivity

1. Group membership, keenness, leadership and sense of responsibility,
2. Group capacity and level of confidence,
3. Status of financial capital base,

4. External linkages, both vertical and horizontal, and
5. Technologies and improvement.

The generic criterion for measuring 'equity' includes criteria, such as making sense of group objectives by all its members and active participation of members in decision-making. When group-based activities are broad-based, they help in creating space for participation of poor and the marginalised women and men. The change is from participation by a few members to participation by many. An important issue in equity is who benefits from group-based activities. For the poor and the weak, the livelihood impacts of group-based activities are crucial for reducing the vulnerabilities they face. It is with inclusion of poor and marginalised people that local management of natural resources become more meaningful. The criteria considered for reflecting 'equity' in measurement of social capital are as follows.

Criteria for Equity

1. Broad-based understanding of group activities and worldview;
2. Group participation in decision-making;
3 Equity in benefit-flows; and
4. Livelihood impacts and reduction in vulnerabilities.

The generic criterion for measuring 'sustainability' includes criteria, which promote sustenance and continuity of group efforts, help in recouping from vulnerable situations, in maintaining assets and capital stocks for future. A group, which has vision for the future can evolve a group strategy. A loosely knit group is less cohesive as compared to a group, which is more compact with inner norms, mutual trust and faith. Role clarity helps to lessen conflicts. Ownership feelings for one's group improve prospects of sustainability. The more is the ability of the group to raise issues and resolve conflicts the better are the chances for the group staying together. Regular maintenance of assets by group is also an important indicator of sustainability. The criteria for measuring 'sustainability' aspects are as follows.

Criteria for Sustainability

1. Vision/Ideas for future;
2. Group-based natural resource regeneration/conservation;
3. Internal norms, mutual trust and role clarity;

4. Group attachment/ownership;
5. Ability to raise issues and resolve conflict; and
6. Maintenance of asset.

Measure of Social Capital in Forest Protection Committees, Midnapore

JFM is a major initiative towards local community involvement in State Forestry. Experience in JFM holds important lessons for collaborative exercises in natural resource management. As lesser partners in collaboration, the local communities offer services for protection of forest and are entitled to a trivial share of timber production (generally 25 per cent of the total) though gain access to minor forest produce such as fuel wood, fodder etc. The four villages under study are located in the South of Midnapore District, near forest areas in the Kalaikunda forest range, which covers three beats, Sankrail, Bardanga and Kalaikunda. While the villages Mulbandh, Tungadhua and Geriashuli covered in this study are in the Kalaikunda beat, village Duganhari is in the Sankrail beat. Participatory Rural Appraisal (PRA) sessions (Mukherjee, 2001) held in the four villages during 1999 provides basis for estimation of social capital in the FPC's of these villages. The villages selected were based on local people's views about success and failure stories in JFM in the Kalaikunda forest range.

Joint Forest Management at Durganhari

The Durganhari (Sankrail) FPC area started in 1998 with coverage of 502 hectares. It had a total of 15 *mouza*'s and 910 members. Earlier, the forest had turned into a barren land. In this village there were 90 households of which 30 were women-headed households. There were not many sources of livelihoods within the village. There was acute shortage of water in this village. The beat officer went and talked to a few villagers for initiating JFM. The response from the local Panchayat was positive and in a month's time the Panchayat helped the community to come forward and organize themselves for protection of local forest. There was underlying situation of conflict in the community and many women and men were not convinced about protection of local forest as a group. For many others the forest was a critical source of livelihood and protection of forest had an accompanying cost, especially for women-headed households with young children. Benefits from the forest included collecting dead and dry leaves for fuel at home and also selling them at the rate of Rs. 2 per gunny bag. Some women were also stitching Sal leaves and getting Rs. 20 per 1000 leaves. Some were cutting trees and selling them. The Forest Department had constructed a well 5 years back in 1993, which became dysfunctional without maintenance. The local forest plantation was mainly in terms of Sal forest with some Eucalyptus trees. Sal forest needed considerable care and maintenance. The level of social capital was low with poor maintenance of assets created and inability of the group to resolve conflicts within themselves as well as with the Forest Department. The group was loosely formed with low cohesiveness and little clarity of purpose and group norms.

JFM at Geriashuli

Village Geriashuli (Kalaikunda) has 180 households, where JFM started in 1992 covering an area of 107.35 hectare. The *mouza* villages under the local FPC were Deonmaro, Koriyasul, Monlisool, Dyinmari, Geriashuli. The species planted were Eucalyptus, '*Chhattim*', Neem, '*Subabul*', Mango, Jackfruit, Cashew and Fire of the forest. The villagers of Geriashuli made two women responsible for forest protection though many villagers were not convinced about community's role in protecting forest. The two women guards went to the forest daily and they were given 25/30 kg of rice every month for guarding the forest. For the years 1992-95 the forest growth was quite good and well maintained. The beat officer advised the FPC from time to time. The forest was protected with much care and no body caused any harm to the trees. With change in the beat officer there was marked fall in official interest of the Forest Department. Illicit felling of trees gathered momentum in the second half of 1996-97.

Those villagers who were not convinced about protection of the local forest raised their heads in 1996 and unity amongst FPC members weakened. The FPC with no powers to impose and recover penalty and with questionable legitimacy was unable to settle inner conflicts and fight the negligence of the Department. Alarmed by the rapid destruction of the forest, the FPC made a proposal and sent it to the DFO for quick felling of the forest under JFM. But they were told that the committee should be looking after the forest for at least 5 years. One issue raised by the village group was that when FPC was entrusted protection of the forest then why the Forest Department was not sharing the cash earned through imposition of fines. If the villagers get their share they feel encouraged. They also said that the rules regarding forest protection need to be imposed strictly and the value of penalty/fine should be increased. Some thieves need to be arrested and put behind bars. Some FPC members were of the opinion that the Forest department should find different ways to raise awareness about JFM and also listen to FPC. Awareness-raising of peo ple about the utility of the forest and the objectives of FPC are also important. The laws need to be more flexible. The FPC had no record or official paper on JFM-related contract/MOU, on official funds spent and on trees planted though they protected the forest and raised funds for the women guards and protected the forest. In general, the problem of food-livelihood insecurity was rampant and options for livelihood limited.

JFM at Mulbandh

Village Mulbandh with 80 households (10-12 women-headed households), around 10 km off the metal road had an interior location and collaborated for JFM in 1988. Its FPC contributed towards growth of the local forest, whereby the local fuel wood situation improved. The community was well aware about the objectives of JFM and looked forward to their share in timber when the forest would fructify. However, the Forest Department made considerable delay in felling of trees under JFM due to backlog of its felling activities. The situation of the local forest in Mulbandh was such that even when some illicit felling took place the forest had plenty to meet the local fuel requirements, though the community felt shortage of wood for construction purposes.

The experience under JFM was productive as compared to the earlier experience of the local community when their own forest disappeared and they were forced to go to other forests for minor forest products. That was not a pleasant experience. Under the JFM, the local women were free to collect fuel wood and leaves from the local forest, which saved time. Earlier they spent 2 to 3 hours to collect fuel wood and twigs from other areas. With growth in their local forest it was much easier and quicker and with dignity. The dry twigs were used for cooking rice while the dry leaves were used for boiling paddy. They were able to sell dry leaves as fuel at Rs. 5 a jute bag while a bag full of dry twigs was sold at Rs. 10 per bag. They collected mushrooms from the forest during rainy season and sold some of it. They grazed their cows and goats. They also ate cashew nuts collected from the forest and sold them as well. Since, they are unable to protect the forest on a daily basis some felling took place. One benefit perceived was the income expected from harvesting of trees under JFM. The women formed a group and visited distant ponds to access alternate sources of livelihoods. The local women and men thought that the nature of work of the Forest Department had changed considerably with JFM. The Department's role was advising FPC from time to time, patrolling, sorting out land-related issues, arranging meetings with community members, collecting fines etc.

JFM at Tungadhua

There were 110 households in village Tungadhua (near Jhargram, Sub-division Sankrail), of which 50 per cent were poor. JFM was initiated in December 1990 in the local forest near Tungadhua covering an area of 40 hectare. The species were Eucalyptus, '*Manjari*', Sal etc. The local villagers mentioned about lessons learnt from their earlier experience of acute fuel crisis. Prior to plantation under JFM, there was dense forest around Tungadhua, which gradually disappeared over time. The women were forced to walk 10 to 12 km per day and still were unable to find enough fuel and fodder.

On behalf of the Forest Department, the Ramakrishna Lok Shiksha Parishad, an NGO, came to explain to them about JFM. This helped in raising awareness and social motivation. The local community became aware about the utility of protecting forests. Other departments were also invited, e.g. animal husbandry, public health engineering, veterinary doctor for there was acute scarcity of services. For the sake of JFM the community guarded the forest at night. Fine/penalty imposed to prevent illicit felling yielded results. The women felt motivated and encouraged for they enjoyed tangible benefits from the forest. The local people also protected the forest from fire. There was rotational felling of every 20 ha per year where poor were involved. The total area of the forest was 40 hectares, of which 20 hectares were felled in 1997 and 18 hectares in 1998. Everybody got equal share of money from harvesting trees under JFM. The first time they got the money was on 22 March 1998. They were able to get dry leaves for fuel purposes from the forest on a daily basis. The villagers also kept the thieves away especially during the deficit months of *Bhadra, Aswin* and *Kartick.* In *Jyaistha,* they collected and sold Sal seeds/fruits at Rs. 5/10 a kg. They also sold Sal leaves in *Chaitra, Baisakh, Jyaistha* at Rs. 40 per 1000 leaves. During rainy season, they collected mushrooms from the forest, and also sold them at times for Rs. 15/20 per kg. They collected wild potato, which they ate. They also collected fruits like *Piyal* and *Kendu*, leaves of the latter used for making "bidis". Date leaves and date also grew. Sometimes they spotted animals in the forest like rabbit, jackals, one or two leopards, wild cat, snakes, elephants and birds.

With regard to the future they wanted to plant some crops, which could grow underneath the soil such as turmeric and ginger. Some good timber like Segun could be grown for value addition. Growing of Sal trees in the forest was also considered important because from good growth of Sal trees, seeds and leaves can be collected and "Dhuna" will also be available. The villagers thought that it was possible to cultivate honey in the forest. They opined that all wastelands in the village should be converted to social forestry.

Some plantation on private wastelands and attempts at soil conservation was being made. With acute shortage of water plantation was a problem. FPC put restriction on a seasonal basis during acute scarcity period around *Aswin* and *Chaitra.* Training in NTFP collection and processing was given to some whc came back and started a discussion group after which a demonstration plot was selected and whose results were assessed. The village committee had decided that there should be imposition of fine on those people who cut the trees and the costs realised. They were also in favour of planting new trees against tree felled illicitly. There was shortage of gadgets such as battery, torch required for protection. Species were to be planted as per the villagers' choice.

Findings

Mere establishment of institutions does not guarantee that localized natural resources will be managed in a sustainable manner. The process of social capital formation is important for it holds the key to collective achievement of common goals and objectives by community/group. Increase in social capital of an institution is critical for achievement of its objectives in a sustainable manner. Table 1.1 provides a glimpse of the measures of social capital estimated for the four FPC's under consideration. Scores on the criteria for measurement of social capital show that at least two criteria, one "status of financial capital" and two, "technologies and improvement" were not considered important for JFM and hence had lowest score of '1'. Scores on other criteria varied across committees.

Durganhari FPC was relatively new and its measure of social capital was 16.7 on 100 as shown in Table 1.1. It had teething problems where the local community members were not convinced about JFM and had not made enough sense of JFM, which was virtually imposed on them. Activities offsetting vulnerabilities in livelihoods for women dependent on forest were not properly integrated with forest protection. It is important to mention that social capital does not increase in vacuum. It requires enabling conditions such as increased awareness of communities, increase in mutual trust and faith of group members, alternate options for livelihoods, empowerment in terms of resolving conflicts etc. Such conditions were non-existent in Durganhari FPC.

Table 1.1: Measurement of Social Capital of Forest Protection Committee. Joint Forest Management, Midnapore (West Bengal)

Measurement Criteria of Social Capital	FPC-Village Durganhari (Initial Year: 1998)	FPC-Village Geriashuli (Initial Year: (1992)	FPC-Village Mulbandh (Initial Year: 1988)	FPC-Village Tungadhua (Initial Year: 1990)
1	2	3	4	5
Productivity				
1. Group membership, keenness, leadership and sense of responsibility	1	1	3	4
2. Group capacity and level of confidence	1	1	3	4
3. Status of financial capital base	1	1	1	2
4. External linkages—vertical and horizontal	1	1	2	2
5. Technologies and improvement	1	1	1	1
Equity				
6. Broad-based understanding of group activities and worldview	1	2	3	4
7. Group participation in decision-making	1	1	2	2
8. Equity in benefit-flows	1	1	4	4
9. Livelihood impacts and reduction in vulnerabilities	1	1	5	2
Sustainability				
Vision/Ideas for future	1	1	3	4
Group-based natural resource regeneration/conservation	1	1	4	4

Contd.......

Table 1.1 *(Contd.)*

1	2	3	4	5
Internal norms, mutual trust and role clarity	1	1	3	4
Group attachment/ownership	1	1	2	3
Ability to raise issues and resolving conflict	1	1	2	3
Maintenance of asset (s)	1	1	3	4
Total score	15/90	16/90	41/90	47/90
Total score on 100	16.7	17.8	45.5	52.2

Note 1: Qualitative Scoring: 1 = Negligible; 2 = Low; 3 = Medium; 4 = High; 5 = Very High; 6 = Excellent.

Note 2: There are 15 criteria for measurement. Each criteria with the highest score of 6, leads to a total score of 90. Any group or people's committee, which scores "excellent" on all criteria has a total score of 90 (6 multiplied by 15) while that, which scores "negligible" on all criteria has a total score of 15 (1 multiplied by 15).

Source: Data based on PRA-type sessions held at Durganhari, Geriashuli, Tungadhua and Mulbandh villages with local women and men groups.

For Geriashuli FPC, social capital was estimated at a low figure of 17.8 on 100, which is quite comparable to that of Durganhari FPC, though the latter committee was formed six years later. Geriashuli FPC started in 1992, however, its position on social capital made negligible progress with low scores on most of the criteria as shown in Fig. 1.1 Though at first the community came together with active support of the Forest Department, the under-currents of inner group conflicts remained very much in existence and could not be sorted out amicably. Later with change of staff, the Forest Department became inactive in mobilising community members. This provided space to conflicting issues concerning Forest Department raising their heads and there was erosion of social capital. The mutual understanding within the community could not make progress with re-surfacing of inner conflicts and their social capital weakened.

The case was different for both villages, Mulbandh and Tungadhua, which had relatively old FPCs. However social capital measure of Tungadhua was higher than that of Mulbandh, which started in 1990. Both had made progress on several fronts and the social capital of Tungadhua was relatively high. Though maintenance of assets, internal norms and mutual trust was higher in Tungadhua community, livelihood impacts and reduction in vulnerabilities were relatively higher for Mulbandh community. Their natural resource base was larger and also the social capital formed helped women to travel as a group to ponds at a distance from the village and catch fish and collect snails as alternative sources of livelihood.

Those FPCs performed better and had higher measures of social capital where the community memberscame together, appreciated JFM objectives and resolved their conflicts amongst themselves and with the Forest Department. In such case the community members made sense of JFM, got motivated, formed vision, rules and norms and maintained local forests. Social capital virtually stagnated for those in which conflicts, whether internal or external, within themselves and with the Forest Department could not be resolved.

The above measures of social capital have important policy implications in terms of capacity building. To start with it is important to find ways of resolving conflicts pertaining to forest as a source of local livelihoods and mutual clarity of roles, responsibilities and powers. Building alternate livelihood options is a crucial aspect of JFM. It implies an integrated approach to forest protection with sustainable livelihoods thereby incorporating role of other development agencies. Of top-most significance are the social skills of external agencies approaching local communities for JFM. Such skills become important for social capital formation. Social skills include ways of approaching local communities, methods for facilitating group formation/institution building, skills for fostering group participation, especially women groups, conducting participatory planning sessions, supporting networks/linkages and identifying ways for sustaining participation, including those of women and other marginalized sections of society. The core values for development agencies supporting social capital formation at local level cannot be under-scored. Such values are transparency and honesty of purpose, respecting knowledge, experience and views of local women and men, listening to the poor and embracing errors. It is essentially a process of learning-by-doing since no 'blueprint' is available for formation and enrichment of social capital.

(Thanks are due to the women and men groups from forest villages of Durganhari, Geriashuli, Mulbandh and Tungadhua, Kalaikunda Range, Midnapore, West Bengal for their participation in assessment of social capital. Writing of this paper was supported by Development Tracks Research, Training & Consultancy, New Delhi.)

REFERENCES

Cernea, M.M. (1991): *Putting People First*, (Second Edition), Oxford University Press.

Mukherjee, Neela (1997): *Participatory Appraisal of Natural Resources*, Concept Publishing Company, New Delhi.

Mukherjee, Neela (2001): *Participatory Learning and Action with 100 Field Methods* (Forthcoming), Concept Publishing Company, New Delhi.

Pretty, J. (1995): "Participatory learning for sustainable agriculture", *World Development*, 23(8), 1247-1263.

Pretty, Jules and Hugh Ward (2001): "Social Capital and the Environment", *World Development*, Vol. 29, No.2, pp.209-227.

Putnam, Robert D, Leonardi, R., and Nanetti, R.Y. (1993): *Making Democracy Work: Civic Tradition in Modern Italy*, Princeton University Press, Princeton N.J.

Serra, Renata (2001): "Social Capital: Meaningful and Measurable at the State Level?", *Economic and Political Weekly*, February 24, 2001.

Uphoff, N. (1992), *Learning from Gal Oya: Possibilities for Participatory Development and Post-Newtonian Science*, Cornell University Press, Ithaca.

2

PARTICIPATORY APPRAISAL FOR IMPROVED PERFORMANCE OF LIVESTOCK

MAHESH CHANDER, TANMAY SAMAJDAR and SANJAY KUMAR

Introduction

Livestock sector plays an important role in supplementing family incomes and providing employment in the rural areas, especially among the landless, small and marginal farmers and women in developing countries in general and India in particular. India is endowed with livestock resources of considerable genetic diversity. Its livestock population (Annexure I) accounts for about 11 per cent of the world's livestock population. It accounts for 56 per cent of the world's buffalo population. Sixteen per cent of the world's goat population and 16 per cent of the cattle population is in India. It ranks first in the world in respect of cattle and buffalo population. While the proportionate contribution of livestock sector (4.8-6.5%) to total Gross Domestic Product (GDP) has remained almost constant (Annexure II); its contribution has gone upto 22.6 per cent by 1998-99. But, the investment of Government of India (GOI) including share of states in Animal Husbandry and Dairying (AH&D) sector is extremely low and varies between 0.4 per cent and 1.0 per cent. The investments in AH&D as a percentage of total investments of GOI in 9th Plan was 0.4 per cent only. This calls for massive investment during 10th Plan (Bhat, 2002). Moreover, the larger policy shift and institutional arrangements at the top level alone do not attain minor developmental gains at the micro level.

So, the policy planning should be done after having the micro view of the area at the grassroots level for which the development is basically meant. Therefore, the livestock sector needs attention from all the sectors of development so that they focus on grassroots level realities. The agro-research institutions, agricultural universities, state animal husbandry departments, co-operatives, dairy federations, livestock feed industries, fodder development agencies, all need to understand the ground realities and need to jointly discuss and act towards sustainable livestock development. Above all, the participation of the livestock owners is crucial for making development efforts effective in the livestock sector. The livestock owners should be involved in livestock development planning, execution and monitoring of development projects taking into account the local conditions, requirements, perceptions, resource availability, traditions, practices, aspirations etc. Here lies the importance of Participatory Appraisals (PAs) or commonly termed Participatory Rural Appraisals (PRAs). The provision, therefore, must be made for higher allocation of funds to livestock sector to conduct research in general and PAs in particular for improved performance.

Participatory Appraisal is a research methodology for interacting with stakeholders, understanding them and learning from them. It involves a set of principles, a process of communication and a menu of methods for seeking people's participation in putting forward their points of view about any issue and enabling them to do their own analysis with a view to make use of such learning (Mukherjee, 1997). At the end of the 1980s, PA began to evolve in the search for practical research and planning approaches that could support more decentralized planning and more democratic decision-making, value social diversity, work towards sustainability, and enhance community participation and empowerment (Chambers and Guijt, 1995). Since then, the use of PAs has gone up quite significantly in many different areas of social and economic activity.

Participatory methods have the potential to bring together information from a diversity of sources more rapidly and cost effectively than any other quantitative or qualitative methods alone. It has a rich potential and offers a methodologically powerful opportunity of which development practitioners can make good use (Mukherjee, 1991). Due to its great potential, PA has expanded and spread from merely appraisal and analysis to planning, action and M&E, from rural to urban, from NGOs to government departments and universities, in the past decade. The approaches, methods and behaviours have proved applicable in many types of institutions. NGOs were the pioneers in PA application but many government development organizations, training institutes, and universities are now using and evolving variants of PA. In some countries and regions, the use of PA has become routine: parts of Nepal, Andhra Pradesh and some districts in Tanzania, for example (Chambers, 2002).

Alongside potential merits, due to indiscriminate use of PA, quality assurance has been a concern for the whole of the past decades. A number of observers and practitioners often express doubts about the quality of some of this work, its potential to exclude certain groups, the way that it has become an orthodoxy or ritual to be followed, and the way that it can become dominated by tools, methods, and exercises at the expense of the content (Mosse, 1994). Many practitioners are using the label without the substances. They fail to put the behaviour and attitude before methods. They are just rushing and dominating in the field. The donors are demanding for training in a day or two, with lecturing without fieldwork, and then implementing in communities as one-offs in a short time. As a result, any approach or method can be used badly and PA provide some excruciating examples of bad practice (Chambers, 2002). It has become a fashion to indicate in the project reports that the PA was used as a method for collection and documenting the data, some complain. Also, it is believed by many that many PA practitioners especially in agricultural sector are poorly equipped in using various PA tools for the simple reason that the training as essential component is missing from the development paradigm.

Participatory Appraisal methods are now commonly applied in various fields, viz. medical, agricultural, organizational and many others. But PA in livestock sector has been limited in spite of its potential merits. The available literature and case studies done clearly show an over emphasis on PA for crop production (Chander and Kumar, 2001), though immense potential of PA in livestock sector cannot be ignored. Leyland (1991) conducted the first substantial review of the development of participatory approaches and methods and their potential applications in livestock development. Ideas from this review was used in a project in Afghanistan which included group and key informant interviews, livestock movement maps, transects, seasonal calendars, pairwise ranking, direct matrix ranking, progeny histories and wealth ranking (Leyland, 1993). Afterwards, PA was applied in livestock sector sporadically (Annexure III). In 1994, IIED published a special issue of PRA notes on livestock, which served as a good guide for livestock practitioners (Kirsopp Reed, 1994).

In India, very few examples of application of PA in livestock production and health can be cited (Chander and Kumar, 2001). The main reason for this is the lack of trained personnel. Especially, the veterinarians are not accustomed to collecting and using qualitative data, and also they have some reservation about the validity of such data (Catley, 2000). Moreover, the governmental agencies continue to give more weightage to the survey methods rather than PAs. They only apply PA if, particularly, asked by the donor or funding agencies. Top-down approaches were followed traditionally to design most of the livestock development programmes on crossbreeding, Artificial Insemination, etc., which often failed to ascertain the farmers and farmer organizational perspective. As a result, the programmes were not as successful as these could have been. Singh and Gurnani (1997) recommended that PAs need to be conducted by a multidisciplinary team of scientists and technicians in all the states to study livestock production systems and farmers' perception, which would help in designing suitable livestock development programmes.

Livestock owners can no longer be seen as an inert substrate upon which development is to be practiced; they are active participants who can and must bring important intellectual contributions to development, if development is to be successful. So, given the vast livestock population and diversity, application of PA in livestock researches is the need of the time for overall development of the livestock sector in India.

PA Tools in Livestock Development Research

There is great diversity in PA tools and approaches along with flexibility to modify them as per the location specific situations. For instance, participatory mapping is very useful and suitable to explore the actual scenario of livestock production in general and semi-intensive and extensive livestock production in particular. It can also be used to explore the grazing of resources, feed and fodders availability, the availability of veterinary facilities, livestock density, disease prone areas etc. It is particularly useful for presentation of information, which could not easily be expressed verbally or in writing and could be used with both literate and illiterate (Catley, 2000).

Ranking and scoring methods can be best used for understanding peoples choice for different species, value of different feed and fodder, different outputs of a species, most damaging diseases, problems and solutions. When there are a number of variables, matrix ranking and scoring can be used. Overall, ranking is a powerful means of comparing a wide range of topics not just by ranking these hierarchically, but also by describing their relative importance. However, a potential problem associated with ranking, and emphasized the danger that ranking data by its very nature allows the use of the standard array of statistical tools, which may be inappropriate or misleading (Roche, 1999). Ranking exercises also have the danger of manipulation by dominant groups, particularly men. The former problem can be solved to some extent by using the QuIk method (de Villiers, 1996). The latter one can be solved by making focus groups (of men and women) and conducting ranking separately.

Calendars are one of the most important tools, which can be used in livestock research. Information on occurrence of diseases, months of grazing, storage of forages as hay, seasonal labour demand, feed availability, seasonal livestock product availability etc. can be obtained through calendars.

Focus group interview can be used to triangulate the information on livestock production. The group can be divided into smaller ones on the basis of sex, age, wealth etc. Generally, the livestock activities are done by female as a result they have greater knowledge about the pros and cons of livestock production. Their opinion and perception are important for devising any research/production strategy and can be obtained through focus group interview in a better way.

Transect is very much useful to give an overview of the farming system in an area. In the context of livestock production, it can be used to discover types and quality of grasses and fodder trees, crops and byproducts available as livestock feed, communal grazing land and water resources (Kirsopp Reed, 1994). Usually, transect is carried out on the basis of direction and topography of the land. Another option in case of livestock research/production could be to do transect on the basis of livestock units (grouped as small, medium and large). A model of such transect is given in Annexure IV.

Some Field Level Problems in Application of PA

Authors conducted PRA for academic research as well for technology introduction and its impact assessment related to the livestock sector with a well constituted multidisciplinary team of experts in the State of Uttranchal in India. We faced some problems in the field and were not satisfied initially with the outcome of the PRA results. Here are some of the actual field problems that we faced in the field.

Getting started: First question which the team faced while introducing the team and the purpose (academic) of PRA to the farmers in most of the villages was what they would get if they participated in the exercise. When they were told that the said exercise is for academic purpose only and the report of the study will be used if required for laboratory research and if they require they will be given a copy of the outcome of the study, they showed little enthusiasm. The team had a tough time to convince the farmers for the PRA. Ultimately, the team had to commit that they will be given free veterinary advice and medicine and for this an animal health camp would be organized, and thus, we require complete information about the existing livestock situation of the village and for that purpose we need to conduct the PRA. The farmers agreed to it and we conducted the study with fairly good amount of participation. After the study we conducted the Animal health camp where the response of the farmers was overwhelming and they came up with lots of query generating useful data to serve the purpose. Many other workers probably face such problems quite often when conducting PRAs.

In yet another case, the team had to first conduct the PRA, before the interested farmers were to be transferred the technology (rabbit rearing) through training. No farmers were interested to participate in the PRA as they were not interested to go for rabbit rearing practices at all. Later on, a group of farmers were brought to the research station and were exposed to the rabbit rearing practices and were told about the economic benefit, they would get out of it. The group was impressed but were hesitant towards getting training and ultimately adopting the technology. When asked about the reason for their hesitation, they told about their inability to bear the cost, which was not true (after the wealth ranking). Ultimately, we had to settle for cost sharing in which they had to arrange for housing, infrastructure and running expenses and we had to provide the training and the breeding stock free of cost to them. They finally agreed to it and were ready to participate in PRA and subsequently sufficient number of farmers adopted the technology.

In the first case, the lesson, which the team learnt was that the farmers have become smart and well aware about their importance. Over the years they are habituated of getting freebies in terms of subsidy out of government sponsored programmes. For purely academic purpose, they do not want to spend their time. As the PRA require more of their time and attention than any other survey techniques, the researchers must take precautions in selecting the technique of the field study. In a new area (remote) where no outsiders go for this type of study, any such activity raises false expectation of the people, which is not good and even may have negative implications for future research endeavours.

In the second case, the lesson the team learnt was that the participation of the farmers from the start of the project would have given better result. If the PRA had been carried out earlier, the farmers would have agreed to bear all the costs and would have given better result.

Transect Walk

While doing the transact walk on the established line, the information which the team gathered was biased towards the crop agriculture as we were not able to observe much of the livestock activity owing to the reason that the most of the livestock were being raised as stall-fed system and were confined to the homestead of the farmers. Even the key informants were also talking more about crop agriculture, as it was their major occupation. The team then decided to try an alternative route for the transect walk. We first collected the information about livestock holding of the village and on the basis of livestock unit we divided the whole village in three major groups, i.e. small, medium and large for the purpose of gaining information on the similarity if any between the same group and the dissimilarity between the different groups. We then moved from household to household identified as different groups and performed the transect walk as per Annexure IV and were satisfied with the outcome. PAs have enough scope for innovations and adaptations so far as the basics are not forgotten.

Mapping/play game exercise: While doing mapping and play game exercise, most of the educated farmers were not comfortable and when asked they expressed that this type of exercise is not suitable for them and they are more comfortable with plain talking and ready to participate in information sharing. On the other hand, the uneducated farmers were enjoying mapping exercise and playinggame and were not comfortable with plain facts and figures like percentage and absolute numbers. In a heterogeneous group (educated and uneducated), there was lot of confusion and nothing concrete was coming. Ultimately, we formed the homogenous group and with the uneducated group mapping and play game exercise was conducted while the educated group was treated with interview. The lesson the team learnt was that the PRA tools must be used carefully considering the background of the respondents/participants. The participants must feel comfortable with the tools so that their active involvement may be assured.

Group interview: When the team was conducting group interview, it faced an unique problem. In the group one or two people used to respond all the time while rest of the group members supported their views although their body language indicated their disagreement. When they were interviewed separately, they came out with different viewpoint. The team faced problem in drawing conclusion and finally, they had to triangulate the information. The lesson was to form a homogenous group as far as possible and triangulate the information source to reach at a particular conclusion.

Variation in gender opinion: The opinion of women and men participants varied on maximum number of topics related to the livestock production. It was very difficult to arrive at a common conclusion. When the team confronted both the groups (men and women) with their counterpart's views, the women surrendered their viewpoint but with negative body language and the men were adamant with their viewpoint. In case of hill animal husbandry, the women, according to the labour/activity chart, were doing more than 80 per cent of the work related to the livestock. Hence, the team decided to take the viewpoint of women in arriving at the conclusion in most of the cases where their involvement was more. This experience only confirms the advice that care should be taken in arriving at any conclusion. The team must observe the body language of the respondents and crosscheck all the sources of the information. One should try to use as many tools as possible to get the correct picture.

Disease Investigation

When the team was conducting PRA for knowing the animal disease status of a particular village along with its economic impact on production, it had to struggle to pinpoint the diseases. The respondents (men) were not able to tell complete symptoms of the disease. When the women were contacted, they were describing the symptom in their own native language (Kumaoni). The interpreter who was a lab technician was translating the things according to his knowledge and the team was not satisfied with his interpretations. Ultimately, we brought different interpreter who had no knowledge about the animal diseases and conducted the interview and were satisfied with the outcome. Correlating the symptoms told by the women respondents was not sufficient enough to pinpoint the disease. The team had one veterinarian and was shown the typical case of one animal and was asked to correlate the symptoms with the disease by observation. The veterinarian gave the general diagnosis and said the confirmation of the disease is only possible through lab diagnosis. The samples were collected with great difficulties, were processed and analyzed, then only the correct diagnosis could be given.

The PRA tools are not sufficient enough for disease investigation of animals. These must be supplemented with lab confirmation. Hence, the team must take the sample collection kit with them to bring the samples for further confirmation of the disease. The selection of interpreter should be done with care and knowledge. Neutral interpreter must be selected to avoid the biases. Sufficient patience must be there with the team and they must learn the things and should train the respondents with their active participation in case of animal disease.

Information Related to Mortality/Morbidity of Animals

The PRA team was not able to collect information about the mortality of the animals properly. The cause and number is important for such study but the farmers were not able to give exact figure relating to mortality of small ruminants and poultry. The progeny history was not sufficient to give correct age profile of the animals. The morbidity data could not be obtained which is a must for arriving at the exact economic losses due to morbidity. Ultimately, we had to go for quantitative type of survey for this purpose to get the figures.

PA should be supplemented with some quantitative type of survey to get the correct figure for above type of information as the policy formulation has to be made on the basis of accurate picture as it involves the life of the animals and affect the disease control programmes and ultimately the economy of the farmers.

We have given a few illustrations, mainly to share our experiences. Therê are plenty of other PA approaches and tools which have their own strengths and weaknesses under different situations especially when we apply them to study issues relating to livestock development. It is not very uncommon to see the difference of opinion in the application of PA tools. These differences are best resolved when actual field exercises are done. Unless one is exposed to the field experience with well-trained trainers, one remains very theoretical, lacking in confidence and skills affecting the quality of output. The development workers who are not trained in PA methodologies at good institutions by experienced trainers would miserably fail once put in a situation where they would have to apply the skills for implementing the development programmes. The authors firmly realize that their performance would have been vastly improved had they been exposed to specific training on PA application in livestock sector at some reputed organization in this area.

Conclusion

There is no paucity of literature on PA concepts, methodology, approaches, tools, techniques and cases from the field yet the experiences from livestock sector are still very limited. The need, therefore, is to try the PA approaches in livestock research and development programmes, often innovating, wherever required and documenting the experiences to be shared with the practitioners particularly among the developing countries, where the potential of livestock is yet to be harnessed to the full extent. For this to happen, opportunities and intensity of training need to be augmented in the developing countries. The PA trainers are now available in plenty especially in NGO sector who can be potential source to train the development administrators and functionaries working with the government agencies and looking after the task of livestock development. There is no doubt that livestock offer vast potential for the economic development of developing countries and also it is now accepted fact that PA has strong merits in understanding the system and evolving means to develop any sector including livestock. The policy planners now seem to be taking note of this fact albeit the pace is yet to pick up. The government agencies have to increasingly embrace PA approaches for the sake of boosting the national economy through improved productivity in livestock sector for much of the governance in developing countries is still with government. The training holds the key towards effective application of PAs, thus, the livestock development agencies must go for imparting training to the officials on PA methodology in big way.

REFERENCES

Bhat, P.N.(2002): *Livestock revolution as a sustainable alternative for poverty alleviation: a strategic approach. Keynote address,* In: 2nd International conference on sustainable agriculture, water resources development and earth care policies, 18-20 December, Bhoovigyan Vikas Foundation, New Delhi.

Catley, A. (2000): The use of Participatory appraisal by veterinarians in Africa. *Rev. sci. tech. Off. Int. Epiz.*, 19(3), pp. 702-714.

Chambers, R. (2002): *Relaxed and Participatory Rural Appraisal: notes for participants in PRA/PLA-related familiarisation workshops.* Institute of Development Studies, University of Sussex, Brighton BN1 9RE, UK.

Chambers, R. and Guijt, I. (1995): PRA—five years later. Where are we now? *FTP Newsletter*, No. 26/27.

Chander, M. and Kumar, S. (2001): PRA and Livestock Development in India: The Emerging Scenario.In: Mukherjee, N., Kumar, V., Jayaswal, M. and Jena, B. (eds), *Learning to Share (Experiences and Reflections on PRA and Community Participation)*, Concept Publishing Company, New Delhi, pp. 73-87.

de Villiers, A.K. (1999): Quantifying Indigenous Knowledge: a rapid method for assessing crop performance without field trial. *Agricultural Research and Extension Network*, July, ODA, UK.

Kirsopp-Reed, K. (1994): A review of PRA methods for livestock research and development. *PRA Notes No.20,* Special Issue on Livestock, IIED, London, pp. 11-36.

Leyland, T. (1993): Animal health care in Afghanistan. *Appropriate Technology*, 19(4), pp. 29-32.

Leyland, T.J. (1991): *Participation in the 80s and 90s: Who asks the questions in livestock development?* M.Sc. dissertation, University of Edinburgh.

Mosse, D. (1994): Authority, Gender and Knowledge: Theoretical Reflections on the Practice of Participatory Rural Appraisal. *Development and Change*, 25(3), pp. 497-526.

Mukherjee, N. (1991): An Alternative Approach to Rural Development—Participatory Rural Appraisal. In: Yugandhar, B.N. and Mukherjee, N. (eds), *Studies in Village India,* Concept Publishing Company, New Delhi.

Mukherjee, N. (1997): *Participatory Rural Appraisal: Methodology and Applications.* Concept Publishing Company, New Delhi, p. 30.

Roche (1999): *Impact Assessment for Development Agencies: Learning to Value Change,* Oxfam Publishing, 274 Banbury Road, Oxford, pp.131-150,

Singh, C.B. and Gurnani, M. (1997): Cattle and buffalo breeding policiy in India-present status and strategy for future. *Technical Bulletin,* National Dairy Research Institute, Karnal, Haryana, pp. 10.

ANNEXURE I

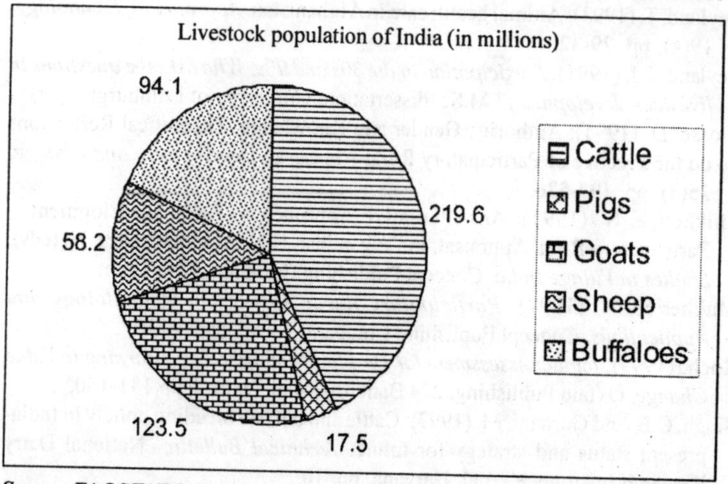

Source: FAOSTAT(http://apps1.fao.org/Page collections? subset=.) Accessed in February, 2003.

ANNEXURE II

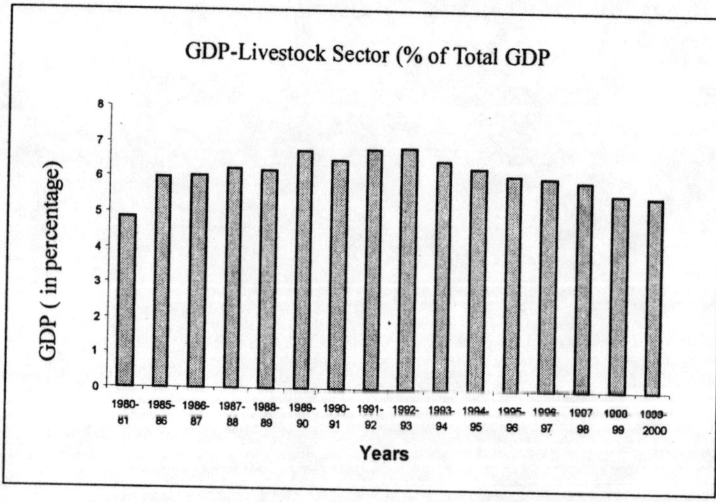

Source: National Accounts Statistics, Central Statistics Organisation, M/O Statisties and Programme Implementation.

ANNEXURE III

Examples of participatory appraisal methods used in livestock development

Country	Notes
1	2
Afganistan	Use of wealth ranking, disease ranking, fodder ranking, seasonal calendars during the design of an animal health project.
Ethiopia	Report which includes a method for 'interviewing cows'. Stakeholder analysis of animal health services based on the use of PA tools, particularly proportional piling.
India	Use of maps, interviews, seasonal calendars and livelihood analyses during an evaluation of a dairy buffalo project.
Indonesia	Outlines the use of progeny histories in a study of economic aspects of malignant catarrhal fever in buffaloes and cattle.
Kenya	Describes the progeny history method.
Kenya, Zimbabwe	Use of wealth ranking and disease ranking in projects implemented by the Intermediate Technology Development Group.
Mongolia	Use of labour calendars by gender; illustrates division of labour for livestock tasks; livestock mobility maps.
Mozam-bique	Use of Venn diagrams to understand institutional links between communities and agencies involved in livestock.
Nepal	Use of maps, progeny histories, rankings and interviews during an evaluation of a village animal health worker project.
Nigeria	Use of RRA to study constraints and solutions facing poultry farmers, comparison of RRA with questionnaire method.
Somalia	Use of PA methods to conduct preliminary investigations on rinderpest in a remote area.
Somaliland	Seasonal calendar showing variations in disease incidence; herders, calendars showing seasonal movements of livestock. Use of participation scoring tools including 'before and after' scoring for programme review and evaluation.

Contd.....

Contd. Annexure III

1	2
	Use of seasonal calendars and scoring tools to investigate tick ecology and tick associated disease.
	Detailed account of a livestock disease scoring tool; discussion on reliability and validity.
South Africa	Outlines the use of RRA within a systems approach to animal health needs assessments.
	Use of rapid appraisal with stakeholders to assess community veterinary needs.
Southern Sudan	Describes the use of participatory animal health surveys from 1993 in the UNICEF Operation Lifeline, Sudan (Southern Sector) Livestock Programme.
Trinidad and Tobago	Use of school essay method and group interviews as part of an ethno veterinary study.
Zambia, Ethiopia, Guinea	Describes a methodology for rapid appraisal, including the use of livestock disease calendars and transect walks.

Source : Catley, 2000.

ANNEXURE IV

Parameters to be observed	Livestock Unit (LU)*		
	Small (< 5 LU)	Medium (5-8 LU)	Large (> 8 LU)
Cropping system Land holding Production system Feeding system Feed/Fodder Housing Labour utilization Gender issues Disease Traditional treatment Veterinary facility Resource flow Water availability Institutional intervention Problems & Solutions Potential/Prospects			

*Cattle and buffaloes above 3 years age = 1.00 LU
Older calves (heifers) = 0.65 LU
Younger calves = 0.35 LU
Sheep and goats = 0.50 LU

3

UNDERSTANDING HIV/AIDS
An Analysis of Women's Voices

MEERA JAYASWAL, KALINDI KUMARI,
R.N. BHAGAT and S.K. SINHA

Introduction

AIDS has become a national threat in a very short span of time. Currently, there are estimated 4 million HIV-infected patients in India this will grow to 25 million in 2010, making India the AIDS capital (*India Today,* 2002). AIDS and HIV is infecting all sections of society-rural as well as urban, men as well as women, illiterate as well as literate, children as well as adolescents, adults and elderly. However, majority of cases (89%) are in the 15-44 age groups (NACO, 1998-99, p. 14).

Medical science is struggling hard and huge amount of money is being spent to control the spread of this dreaded disease. Lack of scientific information, knowledge and awareness regarding the disease makes the situation more dangerous. There are numerous researches indicating that majority of the people in India are still ignorant of the concept, nature and cause of the onset and spread of HIV infection (All India Institute of Hygiene and Public Health, 1997; Natrajan, 1998; Ramasubham, 1995; Voluntary Health Service, 1996; World Bank, 1997).

The most unfortunate aspect of AIDS is the stigma attached to the disease. It refers to the prejudice, discounting, discrediting and discrimination directed to people perceived to be affected by AIDS or HIV and at individuals, groups, and communities with which they are associated (Herek and Glunt, 1998). Stigma leads to discrimination, which is constitutes of "the actions or treatment based on the stigma and directed towards stigmatized (Bunting, 1996). The stigmatized find themselves ostracized, rejected and shunned and may experience sanctions, harassment, scapegoat, and even violence based on their infection or association with HIV/AIDS (APN, 1999; McGrath, 1992).

Many western studies have found the prevalence of AIDS stigma in the population (Herek and Glunt: 1988; Kegeles *et al.,* 1989; Malcolm *et al.,* 1998; McGrath, 1992; UNAIDS, 2000). Pryor and Glenn (1993) pointed out that AIDS stigma is as much as epidemic as the spread of virus. AIDS victims not only fight with the terror of the disease but the terror of the society. AIDS victims are subjected to ill treatment, discrimination and humiliation. The following studies can be quoted as an example of discriminatory behaviour.

- AIDS orphans were forced to leave their former villages (Bhatiasevi, 1999).
- Children with AIDS or having parents with AIDS were expelled from the school (Pryor and Glenn, 1993).
- HIV-positive children were denied to continue schools (Assavanonda, 1999).
- Dismissal from work on the grounds of serostatus has been noted.
- HIV positive people were denied treatment in the hospital (Assavanonda and Hutasingh, 1999).

In the light of the above studies, the present study has been conducted to learn the extent of AIDS awareness and AIDS stigma in the women residing in Jharkhand State of India.

Objectives

The objectives of the present study were as follows:

- To learn the extent of awareness of women about AIDS.
- To learn the prevalence of prejudice against AIDS patients amongst women.

Methods

Some PRA methods applied for the study are listed below:

- Focus group discussion,
- Health ranking,
- Criteria scoring,

- Preference scoring,
- Pair-wise matrix.

Sample

Selection of study sample was carefully made as follows:

— The sample was selected from an urban locality-Kathargonda. There were approximately 500 HH, inhabited by mixed population-tribal, scheduled castes, upper and lower castes Hindus. However, majority was tribal population —90 per cent of the total.

— The main livelihood of the population was daily wage earning and rickshaw pulling. A few people migrated temporarily to Bombay, Calcutta, Delhi, Punjab, Haryana and Madras.

— The locality, Kathargonda was selected because it was within the Ranchi town, exposed to the urban mass media—television, newspaper, cinema, radio, magazines and interaction with the urban community. AIDS was not a strange or unknown term for them. In order to study knowledge about AIDS it is necessary that individuals had some opinion formed by mass media, interaction with people, and/or by any other source.

— Only married women including widows were requested to participate in the discussion. It was felt that the participation of unmarried adolescents girls might affect the group discussion and the women may not feel free to discuss on delicate issues related to AIDS transmission.

— In the course of discussion, the women were requested to state their age, educational levels and occupational status. Their age ranged from 23 to 45 years and they were literate (from 4 years of education to matriculate) with half of them were working as daily wage earners.

The sample constituted as follows:

— Women only—114 in 11 groups,

— Age groups—23 to 45 years,

— Marital status—All married,

— Educational status—Class 4 to matriculate (high school pass).

Process

In the process of rapport building, the facilitators introduced themselves and stated that the purpose of their visit as learning from others about diseases. While inquiring about convenient time of women for discussion, the facilitators were suggested to come afternoon.

Themes Discussed

The themes discussed with the women were as follows:

- Acquaintance with the disease.
- Comparison of AIDS with other diseases.
- What happens to AIDS patients?
- How AIDS happens?
- How AIDS can be prevented or treated, if possible?

Main Points of Discussion

The main points for discussion were as follows:

Acquaintance with AIDS

The women participants were requested to name major diseases they know, have heard about, have witnessed the sufferers in their family, neighbourhood and so on. The women groups listed the following diseases. Also see Chart 3.1

1.	Cholera	2.	Jaundice
3.	TB	4.	Cancer
5.	Sugar	6.	Paralysis
7.	Malaria	8.	AIDS
9.	Stone		

After listing, the women were requested to rank the diseases in terms of—

- What is prevalence in their family or relatives?
- What is the prevalence in the close circle such as neighbourhood, friends' circle and surroundings?
- How much dangerous is the disease for the patient-body parts become affected, severe pain, which cripple patient's everyday life and make dependent?
- To what extent these are contagious?

- What is the expenditure in the treatment for survival?
- What are the chances of being cured?
- What is the chance of death by the disease?

The rankings have been shown in Chart 3.1 and the following points emerge:

— AIDS is the least prevalent disease. They have heard/know hardly one or two affected cases.
— AIDS is highly dreaded disease, affecting the whole body. The affected person becomes weak and cannot survive for a long time.
— AIDS is highly contagious. Anybody just sitting beside; using utensil etc. can become affected by the disease.
— The treatment is very expensive. The treatment include changing of blood quarterly, which is very expensive.
— If diagnosed earlier, AIDS can be treated. Usually AIDS is diagnosed at a later stage. If diagnosed earlier, women think, it can be cured.
— The chance of death is very high, next to cholera. If treated at an early stage, patients can be saved.

What happens in AIDS

Women groups were very confident about the acquaintance with AIDS. They were asked about ways to identify AIDS patients. The symptoms suggested by them are listed below as shown in a human figure drawn by the participants. After listing they were requested to rate the incidence of symptom/s in their convenient unit. The women groups preferred to do so in terms of 1 to 16 annas, 1 anna indicating least prevalence and 16 annas showing the most prevalence. The symptoms in the patients and the scores were given as follows:

- Continuous headache (12 annas)
- Eye becomes red (2 annas)
- Face becomes yellow (2 annas)
- Loses interest in food (12 annas)
- Vomits frequently (12 annas)
- Blood reduces (14 annas)
- Body swells (4 annas)
- Muscles reduces, patient becomes thinner over time (16 annas)
- Face shrinks in size (16 annas)

Chart 3.1: Acquaintance with AIDS—Ranking by the women groups on various indicators

Diseases	Prevalence in the family and Relatives	Prevalence in the neighbourhood and acquaintance	Dangerous	Contagious	Expenditure	Chances of recovery	Chances of death
	1=most prevalent to least prevalent	1=most prevalent to least prevalent	1=most dangerous to least dangerous	1=most contagious to least contagious	1=most expensive to least expensive	1=less chances of recovery to more chances of recovery	1=most chances of death to least chances of death
Cholera	6	6	1	1	2	1	1
Jaundice	2	2	7	5	7	7	Nil
TB	3	3	6	3	1	3	3
Cancer	8	8	2	6	5	5	4
Sugar	7	7	9	Nil	9	9	Nil
Paralysis	4	4	4	Nil	6	4	6
Malaria	1	1	8	4	4	6	5
AIDS	9	9	3	2	3	2	2
Stone	5	5	5	Nil	8	8	7

Participants—Saroj Devi, Renu Devi, Renu Singh, Manju Devi
Place—Kathar Gonda, Hesal, Ranchi Date-10.1.2003
Facilitators—Kalindi Jayaswal and Jyoti Kujur

- Difficulties in walking (10 annas)
- Mild fever (10 annas)

Thus it was found that the symptoms mentioned above were related to each and every organ of the body—starting from head to foot, external as well as internal. Partially it is correct but not even a single woman mentioned about the deficiency of immune system of the body.

In course of the discussion, women shared some of their experiences. Jyoti, one of the women participants stated the following:

> *About 10 years back, a man (35 years old) rented a room. We heard that he is not able to adjust with his family members. Many girls used to come to meet him. People suspected him of having loose character. His body started to swell and after 2 years he died. After death, we heard that he was suffering from AIDS.*

Renu Singh also said the following:

> *In our village one man aged 25 years was infected with AIDS. He had returned from Delhi. His whole body started to loose weight. His blood was also reduced. He went to hospital and was diagnosed as having AIDS. After 2 years, he died.*

Magdali mentioned the following:

> *In our hamlet, a man had AIDS. He became very thin. Within 2 years he died. He left his wife who is becoming thin gradually. She does not talk with anyone. We presume that she will die shortly.*

How AIDS infection occurs?(Etiology of AIDS)

The women participants suggested many causes of AIDS. The list is presented in Chart 3.2. The women were also requested to rate the causes in terms of their convenience. The women groups rated them in terns of 1 anna to 16 annas, where 1 anna indicating least responsible and 16 annas showing the most responsible cause for AIDS disease to occur. For the convenience of discussion, the causes have been grouped under the following broad categories.

Blood and body fluid related contact

- Blood contact
- Blood transfusion
- Needle piercing
- Blood becoming impure
- Insect originating in the contaminated blood
- HIV positive in blood
- Contact through sweating
- Breast feeding
- Contact through urine and spitting
- Contact through eating remains of food (saliva contact)

Air contact through the patient's

- Sneezing
- Respiration
- Cough
- Talking

Physical contact or proximity

- Sharing room
- Eating together
- Sitting together anywhere—cinema hall, home etc.
- Sleeping together
- Shaking hands
- Playing with AIDS affected children
- Kissing
- Embracing
- In mothers womb
- Lap of the infected mother
- Sexual relationship
- Through Flies

Sharing and using materials used by AIDS patients

- Using the bed of AIDS patients
- Sharing toilet
- Sharing cloths
- Sharing tooth brush
- Sharing utensils
- Sharing soap
- Sharing combs

- Using AIDS patient's shaving kits
- Using ear piercing tools used by AIDS patients
- Sharing shoe/boots
- Children playing with syringes used on AIDS patients
- Common toilet
- Through barber
- Through washerman

Thus we find that the women groups have many wrong beliefs about the causes of AIDS. Though some of the causes listed by the women groups are correct such as blood contact, sexual relation and mother to child proximity there are many wrong beliefs that the women group have about AIDS.

How to Prevent AIDS?

About preventing AIDS, there is lack of awareness amongst the sampled women groups. Most of the preventive steps suggested by the women groups as in Chart 3.3 are associated with eliminating the causative factors. The steps have been grouped as follows.

Blood related

- The blood of AIDS patients should not be touched.
- The blood of AIDS patients should be exchanged twice a year.
- AIDS patients should not be allowed to donate blood.
- The blood of family members of the AIDS patients should be tested regularly.
- Syringe, used by the AIDS patients should be thrown away, must not be used by another person.
- Blood should be checked for AIDS insect before transfusion.

Physical contact or proximity with the AIDS patients should be cut totally

Adult men and women in the family

- AIDS patients should be kept in separate room in the family.
- If possible, AIDS patients should be shifted to hospital.
- Women members should not be allowed to cook.
- AIDS affected mothers should not breast feed her child, other healthy person should rear the child.
- AIDS affected women should not conceive, if they have conceived, they should abort pregnancy.

- AIDS patients should not do physical contact, touching, sleeping, sitting, shaking hands.
- AIDS patients should not be allowed to marry.
- There should not be any sexual relationship with AIDS patients.
- Condom should be used during sexual relationship.

Children

- AIDS affected infants and children should have separate sleeping cot.
- The cloths, utensils etc. should be kept separately.
- School going children having AIDS should continue their education but their status should be disclosed to the teacher and other children so that they maintain precaution.

Healthy persons should not share materials used by AIDS patients

- A healthy person should not share bed, clothes, towels, bed covers/sheets, combs, sleeper, shoes and utensils used by AIDS patients.

Community

- If a teacher is suffering from AIDS, he must be forced to resign from his duty.
- If the shopkeeper has AIDS, people should not purchase materials from his shop. However if there is no alternative, wet materials, such as oil must not be purchased at any cost.
- There should be no sexual relationship with call girls.

Others

Nutritious diet can prevent AIDS.

As indicated above, the women groups revealed negative attitude towards AIDS. The groups preferred the following:

- Denial and restriction on family security on grounds of AIDS.
- Mandatory testing.
- Non-confidentiality in disclosing names of persons having AIDS.
- Dismissal from service on grounds of AIDS.

However the women groups were not in favour of denying access to education for AIDS-infected children on the grounds of AIDS.

Chart 3.2 : How AIDS spreads?

Modes of transmission	Number of stones	Criteria scoring	Preference 🔴 Most responsible agent causing AIDS 🔵 Second 🟢 Third	Preferential Scoring 🔴 =3 🔵 =2 🟢 =1
AIDS is spread through the blood of the affected person	● ● ● ● ● ● ● ● ● ● ● ● ● ● ● ●	16	🔴 🔴 🟢 🔴 🔴 🔴 🟢 🟢	19
The injection (needle) used in an AIDS patient is reused to inject a common man.	● ● ● ● ● ● ● ● ● ● ● ● ● ● ● ●	16	🔴 🔴 🟢 🔴	10
AIDS can be spread by talking with AIDS infected person.	● ● ● ● ● ● ● ● ● ● ● ● ● ● ● ●	16	🔴 🟢 🟢 🔵 🔴 🟢 🟢	12
AIDS can be spread by sitting with an AIDS patients.	● ●	2	🟢 🟢 🟢 🔵	5
Taking meal with an AIDS infected person.	● ● ●	3	🟢 🟢 🟢 🔵	5
By using of cloths, towels, combs, foot wears, shoes of the AIDS-infected person.	● ● ● ● ● ● ● ● ● ● ● ● ● ● ● ●	16	🔴 🔴 🔵 🔵 🟢	11
The using of utensils, which were used by an AIDS-injected person.	● ● ● ● ● ● ● ●	8	🟢 🟢 🔵 🔵	6
AIDS can be spread if the infected person is coughing in front of healthy person.	● ● ● ● ● ● ● ● ● ● ● ● ● ● ● ●	16	🔴 🔴 🟢 🟢 🔵 🔵	12
Children, whose mothers are affected, can also get infection.	● ● ● ● ● ● ● ● ● ● ● ● ● ● ● ●	16	🔴 🟢 🔵 🔵	8
AIDS can be spread by shaking hands with AIDS infected person.	● ●	2	🟢 🟢 🔵 🔵	6
The remains of the food consumed by an AIDS patient if eaten by a healthy person also spreads AIDS.	● ● ● ● ● ● ● ● ● ● ● ● ● ● ● ●	16	🔴	3
Sharing a room with AIDS patient can spread the disease.	● ● ●	3	🟢 🟢 🔵 🔵 🔴	9

Contd......

Chart 3.2 : *(Contd.)*

When the blood of an individual becomes impure, the germs of AIDS proliferate into it and the person becomes AIDS affected.	●●●●●●●● ●●●●●●●●	16	●●●●●● ●●●●	26
Physical relation with 'bad' people having 'loose' character can spread AIDS.	●●●●●●●● ●●●●●●●●	16	●●●	8
AIDS can be spread by the infected blood transfused to other person.	●●●●●●●● ●●●●●●●●	16	●●●●●	14
The spit and urine of AIDS-infected person can spread AIDS.	●●●	3	●●●●●	7
AIDS can be spread by kissing an AIDS-infected person	●●●●●●●● ●●●●●●	14	●●	5
Expressing affection to a child by placing him in her lap, an AIDS-infected woman can transmit AIDS to the child.	●●●●●●●● ●●	14	●●●●●●	10
AIDS can be spread by sharing bed with an AIDS-infected person.	●●●●●●●● ●●●●●●●●	16	●●	5
Children who play with syringes, which were used on an AIDS-patient and then had been discarded, can get infected by AIDS.	●●●● ●●●●	8	●●● ●●	11
'HIV positive' in great quantities in blood can also cause AIDS	●●●●●●●● ●●●●●●●●	16	●●●●●●	14
If a fly sits on an AIDS-patient, and then again sits on a healthy person then AIDS can spread from the AIDS patient to the healthy person.	●●●●●●●● ●●●●●●●●	16	●●●● ●●●	14
Sharing a common toilet with that of an AIDS patient can lead to AIDS	●●●●●●●●	8	●●● ●●	8
If a child feeds on the milk of an AIDS-infected mother, AIDS can be transmitted to him.	●●●● ●●●●	8	●●● ●●	12

Contd......

Chart 3.2 : *(Contd.)*

If the child sleeps with an AIDS-infected mother AIDS, he gets transmitted to it.	● ● ● ●	4	🔵 🔵 🔵 🟢 🟢 🟢	9
If healthy children play with AIDS-infected children, the healthy ones gets infected by AIDS.	● ● ● ● ● ● ●	7	🔴 🔵 🔵 🔵 🟢 🟢 🟢 🟢	13
Sitting with an AIDS patient while viewing a movie in a cinema-hall can lead to transmission of AIDS.	● ●	2	🟢 🟢 🟢 🔵 🔵	7
AIDS can be spread by sharing of soap, combs and tooth brush with an AIDS-infected person.	● ● ● ● ● ● ● ● ● ● ● ● ● ●	14	🟢 🔵	3
Clothes washed by AIDS affected washer-men cause AIDS to those persons who wear such washed clothes.	● ● ●	3	🟢 🔵	3
Instruments used by the AIDS-infected barber while shaving or trimming, can also spread AIDS.	● ● ● ● ● ● ● ● ● ● ● ● ● ● ● ●	16	🔴 🔴 🟢	7
Reusing the same needle to pierce the earlobes of a healthy person which had been earlier used in an AIDS affected person leads to transmission of AIDS.	● ● ● ● ● ● ● ● ● ● ● ● ● ● ● ●	16	🔴 🔴 🔴 🔴 🔵	14
The sweat of AIDS patient spreads AIDS.	● ● ● ● ● ● ● ● ● ● ● ● ● ● ● ●	16	🔴 🔵 🟢	6

Notes:

1. Criteria Scoring—Women groups rated in terms of 1 anna to 16 annas. They put small stones to indicate scoring.
2. Preference scoring—The participants expressed the three most responsible agent causing AIDS with the help pasting three coloured dots—

🔴 (Red dot) — Most responsible agent causing AIDS scored as 3

🔵 (Blue dot) — Second most responsible agent causing AIDS scored as 2

🟢 (Green dot) — Third most responsible agent causing AIDS scored as 1

Participants—Renu Devi, Sugani Devi, Birsi Minj, Somari Mahli, Magdali Lakra, Shanti Devi.

Place—Kathar Gonda, Hesal, Ranchi Date14.1.2003

Facilitators—Kalindi Jayaswal and Jyoti Kujur

Chart 3.3 : How AIDS can be prevented?

Preventive measures	Number of stones	Criteria scoring	Preference 🟠 Most effective measure for prevention 🔵 Second 🟢 Third	Preferential Scoring 🟠 =3 🔵 =2 🟢 =1
The blood of AIDS patients is highly contagious, hence no one should touch such blood.	●●●●●●●● ●●●●●●●●	16	🟠🔵🟠🔵🟠🔵	15
The blood of the AIDS patients should not be exchanged in every six months.	●●●●●●●● ●●●●●●●●	16	🟠🔵🟠🔵 🔵🟢	13
The injection (needle) which is used on AIDS patients should not be reused on healthy persons.	●●●●●●●● ●●●●●●●●	16	🟠🟠🔵🟠🟠🔵 🔵🟠	21
AIDS patients should not be allowed to donate blood.	●●●●●●●● ●●●●●●●●	16	🟠🟠🟠🟠🔵 🟠🔵🟠	22
Condoms should be used by the persons engaged in physical relationships.	●●●●●●●● ●●●●●●●●	16	🔵🟠🟠 🟠🔵	13
Nobody should share a bed of an AIDS patients.	●●●●●●●● ●●●●●●●●	16	🟠🟠🟠🔵🟠 🟠🔵	19
If somebody is in the need of blood, then blood should be checked for AIDS insects before transfusion.	●●●●●●●● ●●●●●●	14	🟠🟠🔵🟠 🔵🟠🟠	19
The blood drawn from the family members of AIDs-patients should be checked for AIDS insects.	●●●●●●●● ●●●●●●	14	🟠🔵🟠 🟠🟠	13
No sexual relation with the call girls.	●●●●●●●● ●●●●●●●●	16	🟠🔵🟠	7
If the AIDS women get pregnant, then she should not give birth, instead she should go in for a abortion.	●●●●●●●● ●●●●●●●●	16	🟠🔵🟠	8
If the AIDS women gives birth to a child, then she should not breast feed her child.	●●●●●●●● ●●●●●●●●	16	🟠🟠	6

Contd......

Chart 3.3 : *(Contd.)*

The clothes and other things which had been used by AIDS patients, should be reused only after dipping them into hot water.	● ● ● ● ● ● ● ● ● ● ● ● ● ●	14	● ● ● ●	10
New syringes should only be used.	● ● ● ● ● ● ● ● ● ● ● ● ● ● ● ●	16	● ● ● ●	12
The syringes and needles which had been used by an AIDS patient, should be kept away or buried into the earth.	● ● ● ● ● ● ● ● ● ● ● ● ● ●	14	● ● ●	8
Patients should take such type of diet which forms his/her blood quickly.	● ● ● ● ● ● ● ● ● ● ● ● ●	13	● ● ● ●	8
Nobody should touch AIDS patients.	● ● ● ● ● ● ● ● ● ● ● ● ● ● ● ●	16	● ● ●	7
The family members should try to arrange single and separate room to the AIDS-affected persons.	● ● ● ● ● ● ● ● ● ● ● ● ● ● ● ●	16	● ● ● ● ● ● ● ●	12
AIDS infected persons should be hospitalized.	● ● ● ● ● ● ● ● ● ● ● ●	12	● ● ● ● ● ● ● ● ● ●	16
AIDS women patients should be prevented from cooking family meals.	● ● ● ● ● ● ● ● ● ● ● ● ● ● ● ●	16	● ● ● ● ● ●	7
AIDS women patients should not breast feed her child.	● ● ● ● ● ● ● ● ● ● ● ● ● ● ● ●	16	● ● ● ●	8
AIDS patients should not get married.	● ● ● ● ● ● ● ● ● ● ● ● ● ● ● ●	16	● ● ● ●	7
The bed of the AIDS infected child should be kept separately.	● ● ● ● ● ● ● ● ● ● ● ● ● ●	14	● ● ● ● ● ● ● ● ● ●	12
The clothes and utensils of AIDS infected persons should be kept separately.	● ● ● ● ● ● ● ● ● ● ● ● ● ●	14	● ● ● ● ●	5

Contd......

Chart 3.3 : *(Contd.)*

The AIDS-infected children should continue with their schooling but under severe precautions.	●●●●●	5	●●●●● (green) ● (blue)	7
The AIDS infected school going children should not sit near the normal children	●●●●●●●●	8	●●●● (green) ● (blue)	6
If the teacher is suffering from AIDS, he/she should be forced to resign from his sevice.	●●●●●●●●●●●●●●●●	16	●●●●●● (green) ● (blue) ● (red)	11
If the shopkeeper has AIDS, then none should buy anything from his shop. If there is no alternative, at least liquid materials, like oil must not the purchased from the shop.	●●●●●●●●	8	●●●● (green) ●● (blue)	8

Notes:

1. Criteria Scoring—Women groups rated in terms of 1 anna to 16 annas. They put small stones to indicate scoring.
2. Preference scoring—The participants expressed the three most effective preventive measure for AIDS with the help of pasting three coloured dots.

● (Red dot) — Most effective preventive measure scored as 3
● (Blue dot) — Second most effective preventive measure scored as 2
● (Green dot) — Third most effective preventive measure scored as 1

Participants—Renu Devi, Anita Linda, Magdali Lakra, Rinku Devi, Rita Khalkho.
Place—Kathar Gonda, Hesal, Ranchi Date16.1.2003
Facilitators—Kalindi Jayaswal and Jyoti Kujur

LESSON LEARNT

Some lessons learnt from the PRA exercises with women groups were as follows:

- There is a strong stigma towards AIDS patients, which is harmful to the society and needs to change.
- Any intervention programme shouldnot only target to provide scientific information about AIDS—its causes, symptoms and prevention but also should focus on attitudinal changes.

The study reveals widespread ignorance about the transmission and prevention of AIDS. The ignorance is one of the strongest causes of vulnerability of those affected by the dreaded disease. Since there is no treatment for AIDS, AIDS awareness programme is urgently needed focusing on all segments of the population—specially adolescent boys and girls as well as youths and adults. Women and adolescent girls should be empowered to be assertive so that they could protect themselves from being transmitted the HIV infection. Men groups should also be involved in the AIDS campaign. This will reduce their vulnerability to HIV contraction during migration.

REFERENCES

All India Institute of Hygiene and Public Health (1997): Five years strings of STD/ HIV Intervention, *Programme at Sonagachi*, 1992-1997, Kolkata, India.

APN (1999): A multi-city participatory action research on AIDS and human rights in Asia Pacific Region Report, pp.1-9.

Assavanonda, A. (1999): Future bleak for young victims, *Bangkok Post,* May 31.

Assavanonda, A. and Hutasingh, O. (1999): HIV victims remain patients in rural communities. *Bangkok Post,* September 28.

Bhatiasevi, A (1999): Orphans ostracised by their community. *Bankok Post,* June 28.

Buuting, S. (1996): Sources of Stigma associated with women and HIV. *Advanced Nursing Science* 19_(2): 64-73.

Herek, G. and Glunt, E. (1998): An epidemic of Stigma: Public Reaction to AIDS. *American Psychologist_43(11): 886-891* Last J.M. (ed) (1993). *A Dictionary of Epidemiology,* Oxford University Press, New York.

India Today (2002): AIDS Mess, pp 42- 50, December 9, 2002.

Kegeles, S., Coates, T., Christopher, T.A. and Lazarus, J. (1989). Perceptions of AIDS: The continuing saga of AIDS-related stigma. *AIDS,* 3, S 253-258.

McGrath, J. (1992): The biological impact of social responses to the AIDS epidemic. *Medical Anthropology* 15:63-79.

Malcolm, A., Aggleten, P., Bronfman, M., Galvao, J., Mane, P. and Verral, J. (1998): HIV related Stigmatization and Discrimination : Its forms and contexts. *Critical Public Health 8* (4): 347-370.

NACO (1998-99): *Country Scenario,* NACO Ministry of Health and Family Welfare Government of India, New Delhi.

Natrajan, S. (1998): Testing positive for ignorance on HIV, *Times of India,* June 9.

Pryor, John B. and Glenn, D. Reeder (1993): *The Social Psychology of HIV Infection,* Hillsdale, N. J. Lawrence Eribanm Associates.

Ramasubham, R. (1995): Patriarchy and the risks of HIV transmission to women. In, M. Das Gupta, T.N. Krishnan and Z.C. Chan (Eds). *Women's Health in India: Roles and Vulnerability.* Mumbai; Oxford University Press.

UNAIDS (United Nations Programme on HIV/AIDS, 2000): *Report on the Global HIV/ AIDS Epidemic,* Geneva.

Voluntary Health Services (1996): AIDS presentation and Control project, HIV risk Behaviour in—Sentinel Surveillance Survey. *Report on Baseline Wave* – Chennai, India.

World Bank (1997): *Appraisal Documents,* India, Reproductive And Child Health Project, April.

4

ENABLING PROCESSES IN DOON VALLEY WATERSHED MANAGEMENT

JYOTSNA SITLING

Introduction

After the devastating floods of August 1978 in North India, the Government of India (GoI) appointed a working group to formulate an action plan for flood control in the Indo-Gangetic Basin. The Uttar Pradesh (UP) Forest Department prepared an integrated watershed management plan and its implementation was assisted by the World Bank under the Himalayan Watershed Management Project (HWMP). The Primary objective of the HWMP was to minimise, in selected areas, the further deterioration of the Himalayan ecosystem and depletion of forest cover, improve agriculture productivity and enhance rural incomes.

The Government of UP established the Watershed Management Directorate (WMD) under Hill Development Department to manage the World Bank sponsored Himalayan Watershed Project (1984-85). In 1988 it was reorganised under a unified line of command, whereby staff from line agencies would be deputed to WMD, reporting to a chief Project Director instead of their line Departments. This had helped foster an integrated approach, although it was still primarily focused on sectors.

Lessons Learnt from the Past

Looking back at what this approach achieved, there were many problems encountered: (Thapliyal, Lepcha and Kumar, 1999)

- Because of the large area of operation, there was a greater focus on techno-economic issues rather than on the social issues. The project had set a number of targets, and so village plans were prepared and designed specifically to meet these targets.
- Furthermore, it was not considered useful to incorporate local knowledge into technical implementation activities. This caused a lesser degree of acceptability of the technologies by local people.
- As the approach did not take into account social organization, techno-economic changes could not keep pace with the changes in social/community groups, leading to unsustainable maintenance of common property resources.
- The top-down approach, and the fact that projects were spread over large areas, meant that local people could not be involved from the initial stages in planning, implementation, monitoring and evaluation. They were not properly consulted at every stage and their involvement in the project did not motivate them to maintain their assets on a sustainable basis.
- Staff members were neither properly trained nor oriented in sociological methodologies for consulting and collaborating with people from the initial stages. Neither did they have skills in organizational development.
- Panchayat institutions with which the project worked failed to enforce a common property resource user-obligations.

The Doon Valley Project

The Background

Prompted by local concern at the environmental degradation in the Doon Valley, the European Union agreed to finance the Doon Valley Integrated Watershed Management (IWMP) with the Government of Uttaranchal (erstwhile Uttar Pradesh). The Project started its implementation from 1993 for a period of 7years.

Area and Location

The Doon Valley occupies 2408 sq.km. The project was to be implemented in the area bounded by the lesser Himalaya inner in the north, the Shiwalik hills to the south, the Yamuna river on the west and the Ganges on the east.

The Working Approach

Having gained experience from the past failures as mentioned above, the Doon Valley Watershed Project focused on a participatory and integrated approach to watershed management.

The primary objective of this project was to arrest, and as far as possible reverse, the on-going degradation of the Doon Valley environment. The subsidiary objective was to raise the living standard of the communities through their positive involvement especially through the involvement of the women. Since people have been the agent of change in the process of degradation, they were placed centrally to the project's objectives and strategy.

The Overall Work Plan envisaged a flexible, integrated and holistic approach. The focus on "village watersheds" represented the area of influence of the village. Selection was based on physical conditions, erosion status and incidence of poverty. This initially met with criticism from traditionalists but ultimately it was instrumental in uniting villagers socially thus facilitating establishment of watershed management organisations at the village level (Virgo, 2001). The appropriateness of this approach subsequently has been confirmed elsewhere in India (Kerr *et al.*, 2000).

The project operated by involving local population in all stages of planning, implementation, monitoring, evaluation and aftercare of project assets. The project activities revolved, around developing institutional, technical and financial infrastructure support. Participation of local communities remained central in the development of local capacity, initiative and the institutions. This provided the basis for collective action through consensus, co-ordination and sharing the responsibility for project implementation and future management. This enabled the rural people of the project area to develop their natural resources in a productive, equitable and sustainable manner.

Initial Training and Orientation

In 1993, one year preparation period was offered for rational planning and for re-orientation training for staff. A local NGO provided a series of Village Eco-system planning courses and training on PRA planning and village institution building. A series of regional overseas exposure visits was arranged for senior staff. Emphasis was laid on establishing a meaningful rapport and effective communication with rural communities specially with the womenfolk. The main thrust was to empower people through quality information sharing in terms of understanding the essence and approach of the project.

The Initial problems faced at an organisational level were (Thapliyal, Lepcha and Kumar, 1999):

(i) 'Top-down' procedures of the existing system were required to be rationalized in this new approach.
(ii) Very few planners and policy-makers were interested in implementation of this new approach.
(iii) Project activities were land-based, which made difficulties in assisting landless/small-marginal farmers.
(iv) De-conditioning of communities was needed from past exposure to development on participation.
(v) Congruent social change was time consuming.
(vi) There was low revolving fund for sustainable management of project assets.
(vii) There was poor co-operation from the line agencies.

Planning Phase with a Clear Purpose

During the planning stage the natural resource base and its importance were objectively explained to the community through watershed approach before implementing the project. Once the villagers understood the essence of the project, they engaged themselves in decision-making for participatory activities. Entry point activity had to be undertaken only in those villages taken up in the initial 2 years of the project. In the villages taken up from the 3rd year, test activities were taken up normally at the initial stage of the first year of implementation before taking up any major investment.

The initial agreement reached with the people was as follows:

- Any contribution of the project that met the immediate needs of the villagers was clearly defined and linked to obligation for maintenance.
- Linking of assets provided to the villagers was made with negotiations for reciprocity during field implementation of the conservation practices.
- Equitable sharing of benefits was emphasized.
- Provision of labour in time, mode of payment and sharing of cost for implementing the work before the implementation is agreed upon.
- The level of cash, kind and labour contribution of the community was negotiated with the village organisation subject to a reasonable contribution.

The project was to be implemented for four and a half years in each village:

- The initial half-year was for the rapport building and planning;
- The middle three years were the years of implementation;
- The final one year was for the preparation of the withdrawal phase.

303 villages were taken up in six different phases. In the year 1993 the project started work only in three villages but the number increased progressively as the staff gained experience. This time-scale and programmatic sequence of activities for process transfer was made clear to the community from the beginning. This finite period undoubtedly helped to foster a sense of urgency in communities and project staff. As the programme progressed, communities increasingly appreciated the need to take advantage of the opportunities offered, to develop a vision for the future (Virgo, 2001). This enabled people to develop a timeframe for taking-over responsibilities. Respective roles evolved very clearly by the end of the project, which got formalised in the withdrawal plan for implementation.

Integration of Techno-Economic Inputs and Social Inputs

The project intervened with seven components in an integrated manner. Emphasis was given to handle the village sociologically first. Hence a single staff was deputed to handle the project implementation within a village. Thus much stress was given on cross-disciplinary training of village staff so as to equip them fully on technically sound implementation practices. The components were forestry, animal husbandry, soil conservation, agriculture, horticulture, minor irrigation and energy conservation. More detailed descriptions of the project and its components have been given by Berry and Dutt (1998) and Datta and Virgo (1998).

The village staff was backed by multidisciplinary team members drawn from different departments at field unit level who in turn supported the field staff. The responsibility of implementing the project work lay with the deputy project director, as envisaged in the overall work plan.

On the technology front, resource conservation and production technologies that gave immediate as well as long-term benefit to the farmers were given priority. *In situ* soil and moisture conservation technologies were adopted. Technical plans were modified to a reasonable degree to incorporate grassroots needs. Premium was given in integrating conservation technologies and practices with socio-cultural values. Inputs in livelihood improvement devices was matched and negotiated with improvement in livelihood support systems.

Mainstreaming Gender in the Project Process

Traditionally, women are the managers of the common resources of fuel, fodder, water and medicinal plants. But most technical information from outside has been directed to men rather than women. The present project was, therefore, built such as to facilitate a change from male-centred programmes towards a sharing of knowledge with rural women. Initially all project staff were men. This made it difficult to interact with women in the villages.

Therefore young women were recruited from a nearby university and Non-Governmental Organizations to work as motivators along with the field staff. They in turn were supplemented by women motivators, recruited from the project villages. This led to better interaction, community motivation and involvement of women in the process.

The project tried to address women's drudgery reduction through promotion of women-friendly technologies (crop, fodder, animals, implements) coupled with raising awareness and sensitization of men. This gave them more time, support and confidence to participate in the social decision making process of watershed project through Self-Help Groups (SHGs). The SHGs initiated thrift habit, savings, internal loaning in line with the principle of self-help. Special attention was given to education, training, awareness campaign and developing close linkages with the on-going gender-related poverty alleviation and social programmes.

Lessons Learnt in the Gender Front

- Women realised that their drudgery can be reduced to a great extent through proper natural resource use. This could be done only through collective decision-making. Participating in the group meeting was important for interacting, taking decisions and voicing their collective concern/s.
- In many of the remote villages, a fair degree of awareness could come only after 4 to 5 years of continuous interaction with the local women.
- Market-oriented economic enterprises and linkages with the banks could thrive only in the villages located in and around the

lower foothills. In the far-flung areas the value addition in agriculture products and animal husbandry activities promoted their income.

— Women in inaccessible areas mainly relied on social banking than on economic banking.
— Cultivation of plantation grasses and the installation of bio-gas plants reduced the drudgery of women to a great extent.
— Perceptions differed across SHGs as how to progress further. Some SHGs had simple objectives, like promoting thrift habits among women while others were more ambitious in terms of creating livelihood options for women.
— Risks:

- Not all women could be involved in the SHGs especially in some villages where women from the poorest groups could not be involved.
- Many of the SHG members could not regularly deposit savings; with irregular and dwindling source of regular income in remote areas such deposits were likely to decline.
- Leadership amongst women had emerged in many villagers. It requires further support in terms of capacity building.
- The spread effect of training and exposure visit for women had limited impact as compared to that of men.

Village-Based Organization

One belief underlying the Project was that the basis of development and progress lies in genuinely crafted, initially informal but effective village institutions. A Gram (Village) Resource Management Association (GAREMA) was formed in each village in the course of PRA-based planning exercises, with the aim of fully involving the community in the project process. One woman and one man from each household were made representatives in the GAREMA. Generally, GAREMAs had five to eleven members in the executive body in which five were office-bearers (executives) appointed by consensus or through election. The constitution of GAREMA has been fomalised favouring inclusion of women (33%) and disadvantaged people in the executive committee/s. The Gram Pradhan of the Panchayat is the patron of the committee, who would provide the link with the PRIs. The constitution was being assimilated into the Uttaranchal Panchayti Raj statute. This has given a degree of security to the GAREMA, which should help to ensure its sustainability Virgo, 2001).

Process Orientation in Implementation Phase

During the implementation phase, the project was aimed mainly to help the villagers to develop a self-generated institutional mechanism to implement and sustain the project intervention. The main tasks included support to GAREMAs to develop the institutional capacity in framing and implementing their own rules, regulations and procedures for proper functioning of transparent and accountable village organizations. This involved doing continuous research on sustainable alternatives and developing a guideline for the same through training, workshop and exposure visit and helping GAREMAs to link for external support.

Evolution of Federation (COREMAs)

While forming collective advocacy groups for contribution of voluntary labour for vegetative treatment of erosion prone area since 1997, the socially affiliated villages came together to form clusters called COREMA (Cluster of Resource Management Association) in 1999. Since their inception COREMA have been working closely with GAREMAs to solve their cluster specific problems and challenges.

Over a period of 2 years 1999-2001 COREMA grew as an umbrella organization, which could monitor, guide, support and give the much needed policy direction to the development aspirations of GAREMAs. The project did intensive capacity building training and workshops for COREMA members especially for their leadership development, entrepreneurship development, and for external linkages. In such a course of activities they took up the role of facilitator for the GAREMAs. COREMAs were actively involved in evolving mechanism for participatory monitoring and evaluation system and inter-village auditing system, advocacy for protection of inter-village common property resources, resolving conflict and rewarding the best GAREMAs, and promoting production related activities. Funds for doing all such activities were mobilised from 2 per cent of the principal amount and 10 per cent of the interest derived from the Revolving fund of the GAREMA.

Enabling Policies in Institutions

In the initial stage of the project, the guidelines had to be evolved in the local context through institutional processes with the communities. This created doubts in the mind of the people for they were only used to accepting guidelines given to them from the "top" but never developing their own guidelines. Continuous facilitation and holding of discussions for development of strategies, combined with extensive training to reorientate the staff and villagers contributed significantly in changing their attitude towards process-oriented participatory systems development. This led to evolution of five policy documents which were approved by the Empowered Committee (a high level committee of erstwhile UP Government) in 1999.

These documents are:

— *Garema Rules:* Rules of the Gram Resource Management Association.
— *Reciprocal Obligation Policy:* Guiding principles on reciprocal obligation policy.
— *Revolving Fund Rules:* Broad Guidelines for management of Revolving Fund.
— *Para Professionals, Policy:* Policy on Paraprofessionals.
— *Withdrawal Policy:* A macro-level guideline on the withdrawal strategy of the Project.

These documents transpire the spirit of the institutional processes, which could evolve in the context specific nature of villages—socio-politically and environmentally. It offers a tolerable limit of standardised institutional measures and guidelines suitable for spearheading scaling-up large scale government project both—vertically and horizontally.

Enabling Reciprocal Obligation for Building Ownership

The overall work plan of the Project enshrined the policy of reciprocal obligation, whereby the project expected the people to contribute in terms of time, cash, material or labour towards project interventions. This was to foster a sense of local ownership. The reciprocal obligation measures could not be brought into practice until the project activities were reasonably accepted by the villagers. Once the project interventions started getting accepted in the villages, the contributions were progressively scaled-up during 1995-97 by making the community understand the need to raise a viable fund for self-reliance and sustainability. The major considerations for determining the cash contribution from the individuals were:

— Sacrifices made in adopting conservation practices.
— Economic benefits reaching directly to the stakeholders through the project goods and services.
— Pre-exposure to the items and easily disposable nature of items.
— Items directed towards individual or group of stakeholders.

- — Socio-economic conditions of stakeholders.
- — Remoteness of the area.
- — Technology worth of the items to meet the project's objectives, e.g. bio-gas plants.
- — The disadvantaged people were addressed through upgrading of traditional skills and proactive consideration in non-land based benefits.

The contributions of the farmers in kind practically meant following those conservation practices which led to education and awareness for long-term social environmental gains. These contributions were:

- Helping project in castration of inferior bulls.
- Rational lopping of trees and helping prevent forest fires.
- Closing plantation areas for grazing at least for five years.
- Arable land having slope of 30 degrees provided for horticulture tree crops.
- Use of HYV seeds by villagers and distribution to others.
- Planting agriculture terraces with fodder trees and grasses.
- All community assets maintained by the villagers.
- Stall feeding of cattle.

Since the modes of sharing for contribution evolved in the villages, differences were bound to come amongst different implementation divisions. These variations were standardised in the form of Reciprocal Obligation Policy through a workshop involving the stakeholders of all the implementation divisions in 1998.

Experiences Gained

1. The economic and environmental analysis of the intervention changed the whole perspective of the project in the eyes of the staff and the villagers from a subsidy driven approach to a demand driven one.
2. A degree of flexibility could be built-in to facilitate lower contribution from poorer families and some of the items could be exclusively earmarked for the poor.
3. Flexibility for cross subsidy was reserved for far-flung villages for penetration of eco-friendly technologies, which otherwise was difficult to achieve, e.g. bio-gas.
4. Activities like afforestation w hich normally benefited the

downstream villages but amounted to sacrifices of the local farmers in the form of additional labour involved in collection of fodder to stall-feed animals by controlling free grazing was given a liberal view for raising the contribution but at the same time social fencing and maximum contribution was encouraged.

5. Since the cost shared by the villagers were deposited in their own fund, their participation, ownership and stake in creation and management of revolving fund became quite high.
6. The principle of reciprocal contributions engendered a sense of local ownership, favoured local maintenance of the assets and reduced the subsidy dependency syndrome (Virgo, 2001).

Lessons Learned from Revolving Funds

In the early stages of the project, it was envisaged that the funds would be utilised only for the purpose of maintaining or managing common property resources and that their use would commence only after the project withdrew from the village. The rationale was that this amount of time would be needed to develop understanding between the villagers, so as to ensure proper utilization of the funds (Sharma & Virgo, 1998). Subsequent experience showed that it was better to start using the funds during the presence of the project in the village, so that guidance could be given simultaneously to foster confidence. Moreover, as the cost of maintenance of physical assets would incur mostly after the project withdrawal, it was thought that a practical approach was to start loaning out the assets during the implementation period. This helped in demonstrating the potential benefits to villagers in using such funds for general development activities. When this idea was floated amongst the villagers, there was no immediate positive response. However, with continuous persuasion by the project staff, the idea of loaning caught the imagination of most of the GAREMAs and they started thinking seriously on its institutional aspects (modes of payment and repayment; rules and regulations regarding selection of candidates; rates of interest and penalties etc.).

Members used loans for purchase of buffaloes and cows, cash crops, mushroom production, knitting enterprises, raising nurseries, house repair, school admission fees, disease treatment and other essential requirements. The social pressures to repay and maintain the fund proved to be stronger than any external pressure. The revolving fund was the focus of group trisections. The group's ability to maintain records and manage its affairs in turn increased their degree of self-reliance. Villagers recognized the need for legal clause in the GAREMA rules to prevent the misuse of fund, which was being persuaded by the WMD. Internal loaning by the GAREMA gave good results thereby giving greater financial empowerment to the rural people through informal rural banking system.

Sustaining Developmental Initiatives Through Para-Professionals

Keeping in view the dearth of adequate field staff, the project developed para-professionals to enhance institution building process and scale-up programme implementation portfolio. This freed the staff to be involved in training, monitoring, developing new ideas for systems development and other creative activities. As the implementation progressed, the project groomed para-professionals for sustaining the technical extension and service delivery to members in the areas of agriculture, horticulture and animal husbandry. The jobs identified were related to pest diagnosis, management and control, agriculture input supply, experimentation, animal health care and introduction of new production technologies. The project helped the para-professionals to explore their services in a cluster of villages and facilitated to establish their service market amongst local communities through market research and negotiation with the GAREMAs. Initially the project supported the para-professionals financially, but this was phased out within a clearly defined time frame.

Although this concept could not make much of a breakthrough in all the areas, it took roots in isolated pockets, where para-professional gave efficient services through economically viable enterprise for activities such as control of ginger rot, chilly wilt, supply of high yielding variety seeds, vaccination against the prevention of foot and mouth diseases in the livestock, first aid treatment of livestock, in mushroom growing and in pooled marketing of milk and cash crops. Few para-professionals were absorbed by the line departments as regular employees. The withdrawal plan has kept provision for annual fresh training from line departments and priority has been given to para-professional for loaning. Migration of para-professionals has remained a major setback in this exercise. It is recommended that villagers who have the surety of staying in the village or a person above 30 years of age should be trained as para-professional.

Mainstreaming Withdrawal Protocol in the Project Process

After Technical Assistance (TA) recommendation in March 1996, a broad macro level withdrawal guideline was prepared for the project in consultation with the staff and officers which mainly outlined the handing over of assets and responsibilities and the nature of post-project linkages with the line departments.

Initially it was perceived that if planning and implementation process is sound, the project withdrawal would take care of its own. But, field experience was quite different. It was increasingly observed that at the end of the implementation process status of many Community Assets (CA) and Common Property Resources (CPR) had changed, livelihood status and livelihood system of many households had changed, new institutional challenges and new conflict zone/s arose. So once again the members needed to do a SWOT analysis of their institution to foresee all the future problems and possibilities to sustain their institution effectively. This meant preparing concrete micro level plan with functional commitment and accountability of the members for aftercare of assets created by the project.

The plan thus prepared with the villagers was known as 'withdrawal plan' or 'Gram Resource Management Plan'. The plan emphasized adequate provisions to be kept for institutional, technological and financial support system for equal use, upkeep and management of natural common property resource of the village. The plan provided adequate institutional framework within GAREMA and use of its revolving fund. The sole aim of this plan was to engrave self-management by the people in a village system. Since this was a new concept for the project the initial withdrawal plan was prepared as a provisional plan. These plans were tested in the field and improved upon through regular feedback from the community over a period of two years. Need was also felt to evolve a broad micro level withdrawal guidelines to facilitate the other withdrawing villages with all procedural measures for exploring and working upon their future management needs and responsibilities.

Gradually the villagers started developing their own set of guidelines, systems and approaches to operationalise their withdrawal strategy, set in the withdrawal plan. In the first one year of withdrawal phase, the project particularly aimed at capacity building of the community through facilitation in effective networking with the other GAREMA and the line agencies. Other aspects included were community monitoring and evaluation of quantum and the quality of work, identification of critical stages of operation of the plan, operation of timely and fair payment system, setting up of transparent information and accounting and record keeping system, evolution of efficient auditing system, exploration of effective working relationship with the COREMA and liaison with the Panchayat.

A complete guideline was developed through action research based on field-operation of the withdrawal plan in different villages. The guideline took into account the procedural systems and approaches required for implementing the provisional withdrawal plan. It is hoped that all these institutional capacity building processes which need tremendous attention and facilitation role from the project staff will go a long way in developing a real sense of local ownership and capacity to handle the project withdrawal in a sustainable manner. The way communities involved themselves with the implementation of the withdrawal plans showed their high level of commitment to sustain the process project.

Impact of the Project (*Source:* WS Atkins, TA Consultant):

- 350 GAREMAs were formed and mainstreamed with the Panchayati Raj Institutions through the process of social change.
- 50 per cent GAREMAs were functioning where performance of 40 per cent of GAREMAs was satisfactory.
- Women's empowerment was reflected in their involvement in meetings, confidence in decision-making and verbal expression capability.
- The 350 GAREMAs belonging to 303 revenue villages had collected a revolving fund amounting to Rs. 2,63,64,299.00 upto March 2001, of which, Rs. 40,88,935.00 was in the loaning process.
- 297 women SHGs raised their revolving fund amounting to Rs. 20,06,710.00 through internal savings as on March 2001, of which, Rs. 6,11,607.00 was in the form of loan.
- Rural Employment was generated to the tune of 84.42 lakh man-days.
- Fuel collection was reduced by 5 tonnes per family per year. There was saving of time worth 220 hours per family per year.
- There was planting of fuel and fodder species, contribution of rural community especially women for protection and better management of fuel and fodder areas, reduced biotic pressure in forest areas.
- Improved agriculture practices were undertaken, which led to increase of 18 per cent on farm production, vegetable and fruit production.
- Irrigated crop area increased by 34 per cent through minor irrigation works.
- Adopting better livestock management increased income of 30 per cent households.
- Vegetative and engineering structure reduced soil and water loss. Availability of water in the streams increased up to 20 to 30

days in summer.
- Use of Energy conservation measures resulted in saving the time of women by an average 3 hrs and this decreased pressure on forest for fuel wood.

Villagers' Perceptions on Some of the Impacts

- Social awareness for conservation of environment increased remarkably. The villagers own emphasis in keeping lesser number of good quality animals increased. Stall-feeding was gradually adopted and increased.
- Pressure on the forest was reduced due to energy saving devices and collective social pressure. Grass started coming up naturally in the plantations.
- There grew a widespread culture of growing grasses with high nutrition (Jai, Barseem, Gunnie, Napier) on land, both on-farm and off-farm. Increased fodder production, encouraged stall-feeding of cattle.
- Water remained in the streams for 20 to 30 days more in the summer season, which was not the case before project intervention.
- There was rise in the living standard on account of man-days created through employment, increase in agriculture production through irrigation facilities, improved seeds increased income from agriculture and other income generating activities.
- Villagers were able to mobilise collective support for protection of forests.
- Benefits from the project approach strengthened people's confidence in WMD and in the government. Villagers were in favour of other developmental work getting implemented similar to the WMD project. There was the feeling of empowerment in managing own funds in the most needed way.
- Women's involvement got reflected in their involvement in meetings, confidence in decision-making and rise in self-esteem.
- PRIs became more accountable on account of overall awareness that came within the community.

Impact on the Secondary Stakeholders

In the initial years, the government officials had a tendency of being skeptical about the benefits of the project approach. The lead agency's (Ministry of Agriculture, GoI) formal watershed management guideline was somewhat different from the present project methodology. However, lately, the participatory processes evolved by the project became more widely appreciated by both the state and the Central Government funding agencies. The European Union which funded the Project's approach, frequently cited Doon Valley Project as one of the successful projects in India. These changes in attitude could also be due to shift in nation-wide paradigm that village-based participatory watershed projects represent more successful approaches to watershed management in India (Kerr *et al.*, 2000).

Sustainability and Replicability

As stated at the outset (Virgo and Malet, 1993), the participatory approach was a new and at that time, an untested approach. This concern has been reiterated by Rhoades (1999), warning that proof of long-term sustainability is needed and technical issues still remain important. Participatory methods developed by the project have been assimilated into World Bank aided Forestry and Watershed Project in the Himalayan region of India. WMD's planning, management and monitoring capacity is already being used to identify, plan, supervise and monitor participatory watershed and environmental conservation programmes to be implemented by the line agencies and NGOs whether through government or external funding in the newly created state of Uttaranchal, India. Such a perceived need points towards enhancing the facilitation role of WMD (Virgo and Roe, 2001).

WMD requires continuing external support to sustain and expend its institutional development achievements, in the overall context of environmental conservation within the new State of Uttaranchal. As WMD already has a long experience of field implementation, priority in any future external support should be in the area of institutional development and strengthening its facilitation role, rather than for physical project investment (Virgo and Roe, 2001). Impacts of Doon Valley Project may be small in terms of its geographical area of implementation, but the lessons learnt have definitely much wider implications. These will certainly help in setting trends in changing the way in which developmental initiatives are pursued in future projects.

Acknowledgements

The author wishes to thank European Commission. Thanks are also due to our many colleagues from Watershed Management Directorate and Technical Assistance team whose contribution and commitment to this process-oriented approach made participation of the community—a reality in a Government organisation. Most importantly the author feels grateful to the villagers of Doon Valley whose relentless interest and deep involvement in the project made possible all the valuable learning.

Disclaimer

The views expressed in this paper are those of the author and do not necessarily represent the official policy of the Government of Uttaranchal.

REFERENCES

Berry, A. & Dutt, A. (1998): Watershed management through people participation in central Himalays. Presented at GTZ-UNDP sponsored workshop on Community-based Natural Resource Management, Chiang Mai, Thailand.

Dangroup International, (1990): *Doon Valley Integrated Watershed Management Project: Preparation Report* (Request 2148). Commission of European Communities, PVDALA, Brussels, Belgium.

Datta, S.K. and Virgo, K.J., (1998): Towards sustainable Watershed Development through People's participation, *Mountain Research & Development,* 18, 213-233.

Jemes, A.J., Pangtey, V.K., Singh, P. and Virgo, K.J. (2001): *Bringing People's Perceptions to Project Management Desktops: A quantifyied Participatory Assessment of the Doon Valley Project in North India.* Impact Assessment and Project Appraisal (In Prep).

Kerr, J., Pangare, G., Pangare, V. and Gerorge, P.J. (2000): *An Evaluation of Dryland Watershed Development Project in India.* EPTD Discusion Paper 68, International Food Policy Research Institute, Washington, USA.

Fernandez, A.P., (1993): *The Myrada Experience: the interventions of a voluntary agency in the emergence and growth of people's institution of sustained and equitable management of micro watersheds.* MYRADA, Bangalore, India.

Pandey, B.P. and Sitling, J. (2001): *Understanding Sustainability through People's Participation in a Government-led Project: Experiences from the Doon Valley Integrated Watershed Management Project,* Uttaranchal, India. To be presented at World Mountain Symposium, Switzerland.

Rhoades, R.E. (1999): *Participatory Watershed Management: where the shadow falls.* Sustainable Agriculture and Rural Livelihoods, Gatekeeper Series SA81, IIED, London.

Sharma S.V. and Virgo, K.J., (1999): "Developing Village funds to sustain Watershed Management in the Doon Valley Project Uttar Pradesh". *In Participatory Watershed Development: challenges for the twenty-first century.* Ed. J. Farrington, C. Turton & A.J. James. Oxford University Press, New Delhi.

Sitling, J. (1999): Doon Valley Watershed: Making a difference. *Waterland News*, Nov. 98-Jan. 99, New Delhi.

Thapliyal, K.C., Lepcha S.T.S. and Kumar, P. (1999): A new Approach for Government: Doon Valley IWMP. In: *Fertile Ground: impacts of participatory watershed management.* P 157163. Ed. F. Hinchcliffe, J. Thompson, J. Pretty, I. Gujit, P. Shah. IT Publications, London.

Thapliyal, K.C., Lepcha, S.T.S. and Kumar, P., Chndra, B., Virgo, K.J. and Sharma, P.N., (1995): *Participatory Watershed Management in the Lesser Himalays: experience of the Doon Valley Project.* Proc 8th International Soil Conservation Organisation Conference, New Delhi, 1054-1069.

Virgo, K.J. and Maleta, B.P. (1993): Participative Approaches to Watershed Management. Tropical Agriculture Asociation, *Newsletter,* September 1993.

Virgo, K. and & Roe, J. (2001): Why was Doon Valley Project a success ? – Reflections by the Technical Assistance (TA) Team. National Workshop on Watershed Strategy for Uttaranchal, Dehradoon, India.

5

THE STORY OF ANANDAPUR WEAVERS
A District Magistrate's Diary

M.V. RAO

Background

This paper is a case study of a turn-around in sericulture by the weavers of Anandapur village located in Keshpur block in Midnapore District in the State of West Bengal, India. The genesis of the turn-around can be traced back to a seminar organized by the Keshpur Panchayat Samithi, the district administration and Sericulture Directorate to discuss sericulture prospects and problems in the region in May 2002 [on 15-5-2002] at Keshpur. The seminar helped to highlight the various problems faced by the sericulture farmers and weavers of the region. Various reasons were offered during discussions in the seminar and comments were made about the prevailing situation. One local leader put the entire blame for problems on the process of globalization. Due to power looms and spreading of markets, cheaper products were coming from many parts of the country and also from foreign countries, and the weavers of the region were unable to survive the competition, hence the decline in prospects and the poor state of sericulture. The handlooms used by the local weavers were traditional. They were dependent on the local markets for selling their products comprising of *saris* and *dhotis.* A traditional weaver earned Rs.15 per day whereas a construction worker earned at least Rs.50 per day. As their traditional skill was unable to provide sustained livelihoods, they had to look for different occupations. Most of them were working as labourers in construction activities.

The District Magistrate (DM) also took part in the seminar and admitted that his understanding of the issue was better after the interaction and assured the villagers of Anandapur that he would visit the village with officers and bank representatives soon. A brief profile of Anandapur village is as follows.

Profile of Anandapur Village

Total area	= 252.67 hectares
Total population	= 11500
Male	= 6178
Female	= 5322
Number of Muslim families	= 824
Number of SC families	= 495
Number of families engaged in fishing	= 348
Number of families engaged in weaving	= 596
Number of looms presently running	= 35
Number of SHG formed	= 85
Number of Bank Branches	= 1

Anandapur village is one of the largest populated villages of Paschim Medinipur district of West Bengal. This densely populated village was once a famous as well as a busy centre for silk-trade. Historically, the village is home for a large number of weavers. Their predecessors are believed to have migrated from Chandrakona town when they fell victim to a devastating plague. The migrated weavers excelled in handloom clothes, particularly silk based products. Since then, Anandapur has become synonymous for silk in this region. This is corroborated by W.W. Hunter (1876) who observed that in three villages of Keshpur, Narajole and Anandapur of the region, silk production and manufacture were carried out to a considerable extent. Mulberry plants being the best feed of the silkworms were abundantly grown on the Tamal riverside of the region and used by the weavers who spun silk threads as demanded by the silk merchants.

If we go back further into the history, in the 18th century, the streets of Anandapur were said to be vibrant with the continuous sounds of handloom, hectic with the activities connected with silk manufacture. It is evident from the papers of the Board of trade dated 30-11-1803 and 8-10-1809 that Anandapur had a brisk business in silk products. While describing Midnapore Trade Export, Long (1869) states that the English traders installed *Resham Kuthi* (silk industry) at Anandapur to encourage the local weavers and to boost the production of silk fabrics. The glimpses of the histo ry of the 19th century, available only in a scattered form, confirm Anandapur as a renowned centre of silk cultivation and production. History prior to this is not available.

Sources of Raw Materials

The raw materials for silk products used to reach the hands of the weavers in three different ways. Firstly, the mulberry trees were cultivated on the areas adjacent to the river Tamal. The local dealers and wholesale sellers distributed the indigenously produced cocoons among the weavers for processing silk threads. Secondly, the local merchants imported cocoons from areas like Chakulia, Baheragora, Singhbhum, Chaibasa and Chakradharpur. These were distributed among the thread makers. Thirdly, in some cases, finished silk reels, collected by the merchants, were supplied to the weavers.

Varieties of Silk and Silk Products

Of the woven silk thread, the white thinner part is known as silk and the coarse part is locally called *matka*. Similarly, the superfine golden part is called *tasar*, while the coarse one is called *keta*. The weavers of Anandapur designed and fabricated many products out of silk—*matka, tasar* and *kẹta. Saris, dhotis, thaan,* shirting and wrappers were woven in the handlooms on a large scale. Wrappers made of *keta* were very popular and dominated the market. Rose flowers, peacocks and various sketches were designed on the body and edges of the *saris.* The beauty of these products was simply fascinating. Because of their superior quality and exquisite craftsmanship, the products enjoyed monopolistic market in and outside the state. The skilful designs and the varied colours added to the charm of the homemade products.

Markets

Cloth produced from silk and other materials in Anandapur were procured by the local and businessmen from far and wide. The fabrics of Anandapur had an outstanding market throughout the state. The business was not confined within the limits of the state. It crossed the boundaries of West Bengal and extended to the neighbouring States such as Orissa, Bihar, Uttar Pradesh and Madhya Pradesh. The wholesale dealers from Kolkata, Birbhum, Murshidabad, Malda, Bishnupur, Raghunathpur, Bankura and Burdwan crowded the village to lift silk products from the local weavers. Business was carried even through postal system.

Formation of Cooperative

To guard the interest of the silk weavers and to free them from the clutches of moneylenders, 'Anandapur Co-operative Silk and Cotton Weavers' Society Ltd.' was formed in the year 1944. At that time, the society had two hundred fifty working members. The society had also opened two sales counters at Anandapur and Keshpur for expansion of marketing facilities. The members of this Co-operative Society have taken part regularly in different fairs, festivals and exhibitions for promoting their sales.

Causes of Decline

Up to the first half of the twentieth century, the business in silk products went on in full swing. However, the trade had run into serious problems for the following reasons:

(i) The local weavers used to extract thread from the cocoons manually and, therefore, the quality of thread was uneven. The production rate was also very slow.

(ii) At the time of extraction of thread, weavers used to boil the cocoon in warm water instead of the modern method of boiling in Hydrogen Peroxide (H_2O_2) mixture. As a result, the thread did not achieve glossiness.

(iii) The Cooperative Society failed to keep space with the advancement of technology and introduction of *tasar* reeling machines due to their traditional methods and quality of production and hence failed to cope with the challenges posed by better products. This resulted in a sharp decline in the total production of the co-operative society. Due to low profit margins, the financial condition of the co-operative society deteriorated over time.

(iv) The functioning of co-operative also suffered as some people controlled the functioning of the organization. It did not resemble a democratic organization representing members' problems and needs.

All these factors resulted in the weavers gradually losing their interest and the traditional trade turning into a 'lost art'.

Addressing the Problem

On 25-5-2002, the District Magistrate (DM) decided to visit Anandapur and to see for himself the actual condition of the weavers. The DM along with BDO, Keshpur and Pradhan of Anandapur Gram Panchayat went to Balaram De's (one of the most experienced weavers of the village) house and adjoining weavers' houses. The thatched hut where the loom was located looked dark and congested. The roof needed repair. Balaram, about eighty years old had seen the ups and downs of life. He had taught his son, Saktipada and daughter-in-law, Sabita, the traditional art of weaving of *saris.* He mentioned that they sold their products through a cooperative in the village of which they were all members. He could earn Rs.25 in a day if he could complete weaving a *Gamcha* (a big cotton towel). The cooperative paid him the wage. It was difficult for his family to survive on this sort of income. The other members of the family worked as labourers. The loom almost stopped functioning.

Anandapur is also known traditionally for *saris* and men's wear like *Kurta* and *Pyjama* made from *tasar.* They buy *tasar* cocoons from traders of Chakulia of neighbouring Jharkhand State. The rate varies from Re.1 to Rs.1.20 per cocoon. Mostly, the women take out the thread from cocoons through traditional manual methods. As a result, the thread is uneven. The process is unhygienic as they use their thighs for taking out the thread. The cloth made out of this yarn is coarse and rough. They sell this cloth locally and to traders outside the district who make *saris* and men's wear out of this.

One senior Bank official, accompanying the DM, mentioned that he bought a *tasar kurta* and *pyjama* very recently from Midnapore Badabazar for Rs.1200. Anandapur is about twenty-five kilometres from Midnapore. The villagers were asked to calculate the cost of production. Balaram De said that the cloth would cost around Rs. 500 and another Rs. 150 would be added for tailoring charges. There was still a margin of Rs. 500 for the businessman of the town. Discussion centred on the subject for some time. The subsequent question raised was why the end product could not be manufactured and sold by the Anandapur weavers themselves. It was pointed out that finding a suitable shop and engaging a sales person for this purpose could address the problem of marketing. Other issues also started pouring in from his weaver friends who gathered there.

The team also visited Kannailal De's house. He is another weaver of the village. He said that the quality of *tasar* products they produced needed improvement for the younger generation to accept them. The DM remembered having seen *tasar* reeling machines in Malda, in his previous posting. The machines could run on power or could be paddled like a sewing machine. All of them became very inquisitive and were interested to know more about such machines. It was decided that it was worth getting some machines and a training programme could be organised for the women members of the village.

For the past three years, a parallel development process had been taking shape in this village as well as in the whole district through formation of Self-Help Groups of women. The SHGs had become partners in participatory socio-economic development process. Using their own savings and bank credit, the women members of the Groups had taken up micro-enterprises, which were transforming their lives from being voiceless housewives to dynamic partners. Anandapur Gram Panchayat also had eighty-five such groups. Each SHG had been initially provided Rs. 25,000 as revolving fund from Swarnajayanti Swarozgar Yojana (SGSY). The groups were eligible for higher credit facilities to take up enterprises of their choice.

The Intervention

In August 2002, Tasar Reeling Machines arrived in Anandapur. The team comprising of the DM and other officials could arrange the required fund for purchasing the machines from Paschimanchal Unnayan Parishad. The library building of the area was selected for a two-week training programme in reeling. Two experienced trainers were brought from Malda. As the process started, the officials of Sericulture Directorate also got attracted to the whole affair and started taking part in the proceedings. Unfortunately, the intervention and support from the department could have been utilized earlier as the officials were quite aware of these machines. What was needed was sharing the learning and pooling of the resources and know-how. Perhaps, this was too much to expect from a traditional bureaucratic set-up. The surroundings of the library building resembled a big festive occasion. When the DM visited the second day after the machines arrived from Malda, he could not believe the enthusiasm he witnessed. The women were already working with the machines, trying to take out the thread. More than 120 women were jostling to have their hands on the fifteen machines located there. All of them belonged to the Self-Help Groups of this village. After discussion with them and the Panchayat Representatives, it was decided that the machines would be handed over to the groups. While they were there, about 35 women from the adjoining village appeared on the scene and stated that they also needed such machines as they also depended upon *tasar* reeling and weaving for their livelihood. They were assured that they would also be provided machines from either Paschimanchal Unnayan Parishad or from the SGSY Infrastructure Fund.

On the last day of the training, there was a get together of the women, panchayat representatives, BDO (Block Development Officer) and other officials. The DM was also there as he was keen to see their progress and discuss further plans with them. The warmth and affection of the villagers touched everyone. It was as if some perceptible change had taken place in the village. The confident women were showing the fine thread they had reeled from the cocoons with the use of the machines. Some were seen paddling the machines though there was electrical supply for running the machine. They said the speed of the machine was too fast with power found it difficult to control the thread. The trainers intervened and said it was only a question of time and practice before they got perfection in reeling. The women complained as to how ten members of a Self-Help Group residing in different houses could find time and do the reeling on just one machine. The question needed no immediate answer as the villagers had started thinking about the issues at hand.

Nearly one month later in September 2002, the Pradhan of Keshpur Gram Panchayat and some villagers visited the DM for an update on the progress made since such intervention. Surprise was in store as they showed him very fine *tasar* cloth woven by Sabita De, daughter-in-law of Balaram De, which was presented to the DM. They also brought along the previously spun cloth (without new machine) for easy comparison. Everyone could see the big difference. The DM could not resist himself and went to Anandapur the same day in the evening. Sabita was on the loom weaving a new *saree.* The DM asked the villagers why they should buy cocoons from Chakulia when *tasar* cultivation had been traditionally prevailing in many parts of Belpahari, Nayagram and Gopiballavpur of the same district. Curiously, the cultivators sold their cocoons to traders from Chakulia, and weavers of Anandapur bought from the same traders. The role of middlemen was there to see for everyone. He got a margin on both sides, while buying and selling. He bought cocoons in the range of 60 paise to 80 paise whereas he sold at a price of one rupee to one and half rupees. The feasibility of buying the cocoons directly from the farmers of the district was explored which would work out much cheaper.

The Concern

Nearly six months after this, the experiment was on-going but valid concerns were raising their head. Meanwhile, the cooperative also took some amount from the groups to organise for cocoons from outside. The whole issue appeared to be a bit confusing. The DM could not stop asking how much weavers like Balaram De, Tinkari Lekri and Nabakumar Das would earn in a day. Answer was prompt, Rs. 25. One was shocked and also could see the shock and resignation on their faces. It was clear that something seriously was missing in the story. What was needed was the sense of ownership and partnership in the co-operative functioning in relation to its weaver members. It was understood that the concerns and problems of the silent members needed representation within the organization. There was a stark difference between working as a labourer for a middleman and that of working together (or working for!) in a cooperative.

In November 2002, the DM had an occasion to visit Anandapur again. With curiosity, he went around the weavers' homes. They were happy to see him but the initial spirit was gone. They were continuing reeling with the machines with and without power as it suited them. There was acute shortage of cocoons because they were not available round the year. Somebody from the co-operative, raising doubts asked what would happen to the huge amount of yarn produced if it could not be sold. The DM asked them why could not the un-used looms in the village start again. Happily, another weaver, Tinkari said that they had already started doing that. It was clear to them that the margins had to improve and the income had to go up for the weavers to survive. For this, it is necessary to procure cocoons cheaper directly from the *tasar* cultivators. In addition, they had to take up tailoring and sell the end products themselves.

Addressing the Concern

In the last week of February 2003, the DM requested the BDO to accompany him to the adjoining children's park in Midnapore. The idea was to see if a small temporary stall could be erected in a corner of the park so that the visitors could be attracted to buy Anandapur tasar products. They found a small building which was unused. They thought, instead of spending money on the structures, the unused building could be utilised for a month or so to see the response. On 1st March 2003, all got together in a brief inauguration programme where many of the members of Anandapur Self-Help Groups were present with their products. There was hope and happiness on their faces. The first day's sales were around Rs.1000. One week later, the total sales touched Rs.5000. Experience showed that the sales on holidays were more and on working days, less. There was interest amongst the visitors about products and people started giving them fresh orders. The shop did not have enough materials to cater to their demand. Nearly one month after the shop was opened, *tasar saris* and cloth worth Rs.30,000 had been sold. When the DM visited Anandapur again, Sabita was there, busy weaving another *sari* to meet the target. The ambience of Balaram De's house had changed. BDO was also present there and he pointed the noticeable change in the condition of the family. All the members looked physically better and healthy. The walls of house were freshly repaired. Sabita said she was very happy. She was getting nearly Rs. 100 in a day. Everyone's heart was filled with joy. A training programme on embroidery and designing had just been completed in the Keshpur block and the Anandapur SHG members had taken part with great enthusiasm. Seven embroidery machines had been provided to the Self-Help Groups of Anandapur from the SGSY Infrastructure Fund. Five more reeling machines had been provided to interested women from Paschimanchal Unnayan Parshad fund. A mobile sale unit of Anandapur SHG members had also started selling their products in various markets with the help of District Rural Development Cell. The journey of weavers of Anandapur for a better tomorrow has already begun.

Impact Assessment

A. Achievements

(i) The traditional art of *tasar* culture at Anandapur, which had temporarily lost its glory, has restarted its journey in the right direction with active guidance and support from the district administration and panchayats.

(ii) Hope and confidence had been generated among the weavers.

(iii) As the weavers had formed self-help groups, a feeling of cohesiveness and bonding had already developed among them. They were solving their problems on their own in a well-organised manner.

(iv) The SHG members have contributed regularly for generation of their own fund. This has helped them in meeting their capital requirements to some extent. Bank credit has given them the financial strength to buy raw materials and market their products with reduced dependence on middlemen.

(v) With well-equipped training, improved machineries and marketing support, their income has increased. This extra income has also changed their lifestyle to some extent.

(vi) The weavers, who used to toil whereas the middleman would run away with profit, were now working for themselves and their families.

B. What could not be achieved?

(i) A steady and stable market remains to be achieved.

(ii) The Government has provided embroidery training and machines. The weavers of different SHGs should have started embroidery and other works over tasar products for value-addition on regular basis.

(iii) The weavers were generally accustomed to handlooms. To increase quantity and to improve quality, introduction of power loom was essential.

(iv) To ensure steady flow of raw material, production of tasar cocoons should have been produced in the Anandapur area. Alternatively, firm arrangements with tasar farmers should have been made.

(v) Training and skill development in the new and latest fashion designs needed to be arranged for the weavers

C. Lessons learnt

(i) Technology up-gradation and proper skill development training were required for the development of different village industries.

(ii) Formation of SHGs could create the required environment and opportunities for rural renaissance. The SHG movement needed support, strength and spread for improvement in livelihoods for thousands of rural people.

(iii) Actual participation in decision-making of members in democratic organizations like co-operatives had to be ensured to check growth of vested interests and to protect the interest of ordinary members.

An Interactive Session with Sabita for her "worldview"

The following interview of Smt. Sabita Dey, member of Dayamoyee SHG and a successful tasar weaver of Anandapur, mirrors the mind of thousands of such SHG members.

The conversation between Sabita Dey and the interviewer is given below verbatim:

Q. Namaskar, Sabita di. Will you please give us some information about your family?

Sabita: Namaskar. I am Sabita Dey. My husband is Sri Saktipada Dey. Sri Balaram Dey is my father-in-law. Total number of my family members is six. We reside at my father-in-law's house at Palpara in Anandapur.

Q. Please tell us something about your children.

Sabita: I have two children. My daughter is studying in Class-VI and my son is in Class-I.

Q. Sabita di, how old are you?

Sabita: I am thirty-one years old.

Q. Will you give us some information about your parental house?

Sabita: My parental house is in Gourhati at Arambag Sub-division of Hooghly district. My parents still live there.

Q. Sabita di, will you please tell us something about the economic activity of your family?

Sabita: My father-in-law is a famous weaver of Anandapur. Our family is traditionally engaged in cotton and tasar weaving. Besides weaving, we also know tailoring.

Q. How long are you working in this profession?

Sabita: As I said, my father-in-law is a well-known cotton and tasar weaver of this area. My family is working in this trade for the last sixty years. I have learnt weaving from my father-in-law.

Q. What are the problems you face in this trade?

Sabita: We have faced serious problems in the recent past. Earlier, we used to extract tasar from cocoons manually. The tasar threads were of inferior quality and the market was very dull. At that time, we only earned Rs.40 in a day and we could hardly manage two square meals.

Q. What is the present situation?

Sabita: Sir, at last the fortune has smiled on us. Presently we earn up to Rs.100 per day.

Q. Please tell us how the change has become possible.

Sabita: The guidance and co-operation we got from our district administration and local Gram Panchayat has made this possible. As per their guidance, we have formed a SHG named 'Dayamoyee' with ten members belonging to families living below poverty line (BPL) of this locality. The district administration has also arranged necessary training of tasar reeling for us. We were trained on the reeling machine. We were also provided tasar reeling machines by the district administration. Now, we are making fine quality tasar products with this improved thread. Moreover, our group has received Rs. 25,000 as revolving fund from the bank. This has also solved our problem of lack of capital to a great extent.

Q. Can you tell us something about your plans and programmes for marketing of products?

Sabita: The main challenge before us is obviously the marketing. But we are trying our best. With active co-operation of district administration, we are now running a shop for selling of tasar products at the district headquarters. Besides, we will open stalls at G.P. and Block level. We have started a mobile sales counter to cater to different markets of the area. We will also take part in different fairs and festivals on regular basis. We are confident that this strategy will certainly boost our sales.

Q. Due to this economic development, what changes you find in your family condition?

Sabita: Sir, previously, we have never dreamt of other amenities of life. But now, we can easily manage better food and education for our children. Moreover, we can think about the repair works of our house and electricity connection.

Q. How did you benefit by forming Self-Help Group?

Sabita: I can say with confidence that the development of my family has only started after formation of SHG. It has made myself as well as my family economically self-reliant. Above all, it has given me a separate identity and also raised my status in the family and in the locality. I have never earned such recognition earlier in my life.

Q. Thank you, Sabita di.

Sabita: Thank you, Sir.

Acknowledgements

The author acknowledges the contribution of the following during the study and its implementation.

1. Weavers of Anandapur.; 2. Rahul Majumdar, BDO, Keshpur.; 3. Members of 'Anandapur Co-operative Silk and Cotton Weavers, Society Ltd.'

REFERENCES

Hunters, W.W. (1876): *A statistical account of Bengal.*

Long, Rev. J. (1869): *Selection from Unpublished Records of Government.*

Rao, M.V. (2002): *Development for the people: Innovations in Administration,* Subarnarekha, Kolkata.

6

PARTICIPATION AND HUMAN DEVELOPMENT
Bagdah Experience

HARI KRISHNA DWIVEDI and S.B. ROY

This paper focuses on certain aspects of developing such a design, in consonance with the concept of capacity building and social system sequence (Roy *et al.*, 2001) and the lessons learnt from an experiment carried out in Bagdah, one of the blocks of North 24-Paragnas, West Bengal. Unlike previous approaches the entire programme is carried out without any financial support to the community during the entire period of two years when the programme is being implemented. It is in keeping with the paradigm shift that has occurred in recent times in the ways of looking at the relationship of the government and villagers as a provider-acceptor relationship. The participation of the real stakeholders in the planning and implementation of different development and welfare programmes and management of assets and resources has been accepted as the most crucial factor for sustainability of any programme. The main problem plaguing many of the hitherto launched initiatives or programmes for rural development of poverty alleviation or watershed management is how to ensure the involvement of the community/groups in the specific development activity on a sustained basis and keep it going even after the directed project/programme ceases to exist. What steps in human development initiatives and capacity building need be taken to bring continuity or sustainability of the interest and involvement of the community through systematic action for solution of the problems on a long term basis? For the villagers involved in the programme under discussion participatory development is a unique means of direct learning rather than a baggage of intellectual concepts of repeated emotional releases. The programme integrates the body, mind and being, which results in an expanded sense of well-being and an improvement in the quality of life. It is interesting to know how it has been realised.

Empowerment of the people is concretely visualised through a rise in the number of activities with the involvement of the villagers, mainly by the women, increase in the savings, and villagers' greater access to resources, and also increase in productivity. Further, the communities seem to have learnt how to manage their own resources on a sustainable basis. The experiment continues to examine whether the community members will be able to take the responsibility for organizing themselves in the form of community groups, address their crucial problems related to *preventive health care, education and resource management* in the form of developing a habit of savings and income generation. It is expected that if the three basic elements of survival and satisfaction are taken care of, it will facilitate the process of human development. Indeed, human development is said to be a "process of enlarging people's choices, which is achieved by expanding human capabilities and functioning of basic human needs. At all levels of development the three essential capabilities for human development are for the people to lead long and healthy lives, to be knowledgeable and to have access to the resources needed for a decent standard of living" (Haq, 2002). Keeping this in mind the programme of Bagdah experiment has been devised as an integrated effort to link three essential services: health (swasthya), education (siksha) and augmenting Resources through income generation (Sanchay) to help villagers in transforming their way of life.

The experiment in Bagdah is an attempt to initiate the process of community participation by empowering villagers to find ways and means of transforming community organization with their existing resources and manpower thereby leading to human development.

Objective

The objective of Bagdah experiment has been to bring about improvement in the area of integrated development of health, education and resource management by augmenting savings through participation by the community in a planned manner and on a sustained basis. Effort has been made to develop mechanism to ensure that the number of school dropouts decline, the rates of infant mortality and pregnancy related death, fertility rate and 'natural increase rate' come down, attendance in public health centres and immunization increase resulting in greater life expectancy. A sharp rise in community empowerment as well as women's empowerment would accompany it all. Motivating and sensitising both the parties, viz., the members of the community organisation and those belonging to the government is one crucial task in this process.

The Hard Reality

From a realistic assessment of the situation, the authors have seen that despite different family planning/health/immunisation benefits extended by the Health Department and the villagers' constant exposure to health awareness campaigns relating to measures for control of diarrhoea, blindness, leprosy and malaria, the *local people have not come forward to solve their health problems with their own initiative.*

Plan of Action

In the above context, an appropriate plan of action can be taken up, based on field experience whose main points are listed below:

(i) People in general form and work in groups and they do not inevitably spurn change.
(ii) Resistance of individuals to change is overcome through change/s in the group, facilitated by persons with visionary and leadership traits.
(iii) A key step in bringing about societal change is to identify such persons and train them for building their capacity to lead and change the peer groups and neighbourhood.
(iv) To make the change effective in a group and viable in the overall system, networking with other groups in the system needs to be ensured.
(v) Strategic planning is to be undertaken for restructuring the government departments and Panchayati Raj institutions and for promoting and enhancing, among the members of these institutions, the qualities of leadership.

Change in Government and Peoples' Attitudes

Compartmentalization of government functioning is one of the major roadblocks in achieving "Convergence" and "Synergy" in development programme/project at the grassroots. Even with similar broad objectives and the target group, the tone and agenda of these functionaries give limited scope for collective functioning and pooling of efforts. Community mobilization has been found to be an effective means to overcome such problem. Community mobilization brings about much needed convergence at the grassroots level and reduces the barriers in collective functioning. In this task the community has to be sensitised to the interdependent nature of the problems faced by it and to the integrated nature of their solutions and, therefore, to the need for simultaneous and coordinated efforts to achieve the set of interrelated goals.

While we are in the process of convincing the government agency that change is desirable, possible and sustainable, we must convince the authorities further that similar *attitudinal change can be effected successfully amongst the local people, panchayat and villagers.* This is to be done by actually taking a model group and by bringing about the change through a process of sensitisation and motivation.

It is here that an NGO's role can support such change so that members of the local community and the panchayat are effectively sensitised to build a positive attitude towards the solving development problems, in this case related to health and working in harmony with the government officials.

The Mechanism of Sensitisation

To sensitise the target groups their attitude needs to be changed and their vision needs to be focused on solving their own problems in their own way. Below are the main steps and features of the required sensitisation process:

— We must call a mass meeting where the panchayat and health officials are present along with the local people irrespective of sex, caste, religion, and community.
— The audience must be properly communicated so that it can appreciate the importance and benefits of health systems related to it.
— One must mention—how important community participation is in improving the health system since government alone cannot solve the entire problem.
— Once the villagers appreciate this point, they generally begin to understand the importance of the suggested measures and the benefits derivable from them. But, they mention various constraints, which hinder their active participation in health system activities and programme.
— They may voice grievances against Health officials, such as—

They do not visit Primary Health Centres regularly.

- The behaviour of Health Officers is also not good.
- Proper medicines are never available in the local hospital.
- The Panchayat does not perform its duty and carry out its responsibilities.

— On the other hand, Health Officials also generally come out with their complaints that: Owing to their superstitious nature and beliefs the villagers do not pay any heed to any health awareness campaigns. The villagers are poor, illiterate and disorganised, i.e. without any proper leader to lead them. They lack any permanent infrastructure to facilitate their endeavours and also lack proper support from the Panchayat members.

— Similarly, the Panchayat Members may also have their share of grievances. The facilitator or motivator in the meetings involving the local people and other parties must be a good listener, i.e. must be one who listens with attention and patience to all the groups, while they pour in their grievances and complaints.

— When everybody states his/her problems, the facilitator asks the question—"Can there be a solution to all this?"

— Generally at the initial stage the villagers are hesitant to come forward with any solution. However, they slowly and gradually gain confidence and start, one by one, expressing their views. Through this process the Self-Initiated Community Organiser (SICO) can be identified, who will work later as the main resource person/animator to develop village-wide awareness and bring attitudinal change in solving health problems. It is very important to identify a few persons from the society whose attitude can easily be changed towards a common goal such that they are emboldened to come forward in a crowd for serving a cause. Such persons are by nature bold enough to talk in public and value social work and are eager to spend time for socially relevant activities. If ten individuals in a crowd come forward to form a group, it will generate a strong network and the group would gradually replicate and expand. Such volunteers are known as Self-Initiated Community Organisers (SICO) (Roy *et al.,* 1999). Irrespective of age, sex, educational qualification and social status the SICO acts as opinion mobiliser. SICOs facilitate the formation and activation of groups in the community. But, it is not enough just to identify the SICOs—the identified persons must be trained properly in order to build up their capacity.

— Once the capacity is built, the SICOs are assigned some duties/activities, which are suitable for the nature, personality and interest of the SICO. The activities need not be restricted to health only, but also related to literacy, banking, co-operative farming, pisciculture, or anything else, which may be integrated with health activities. The group finally makes commitment towards their self-devised Plan of Action and starts working with a sense of pride and confidence to realise the goals or the objectives set with their own initiative.

— The working process as well as the results achieved from time to time need to be monitored and measured within a specific span of time.

The Integral Steps in SICO Training

— We must begin with ice-breaking where the SICO becomes free of inhibitions and becomes responsive to the ideas and training to be given. Typically, he/she introduces himself or herself, stating his/her background and nature of activity along with his/her strength, weakness, etc.

— After ice-breaking the SICO must be sensitised to come out and state his/her own strengths, i.e. develop and offer the list of the likeable qualities in oneself. They have to be taught how to talk in a manner, which makes their personality likeable and how to build up a cohesive spirit by working with others. This entire exercise is very important as people generally like to follow likeable personalities. So the SICO, himself / herself must firstly be a likeable person. The SICOs also must form a group with likeminded people, i.e. people who share warm vibes amongst themselves.

— Once the SICO groups are formed, the SICOs are asked to do *Visioning* i.e. focusing on a positive vision of things which they would like to happen. For example, the desirable attributes of a Dream Hospital. Initially, there might be some difficulty in visioning since the visualisation might not be very clear. The facilitator must facilitate the visualisation process.

— Once the vision is clear, the question that is asked relates to what are the constraints in translating the vision into reality. The SICOs should list the constraints and generally it becomes apparent that nearly 80 per cent of the constraints are attitudinal whereas only 20 per cent are resource related.

— As the prime importance of attitude thus evolves out, it becomes very clear that in order to solve all health problems, the attitude of the people must be changed and this must be done by the SICOs themselves. It is also established that since people like to listen to people whom they like, the SICOs can acquire likeable qualities such as authenticity, fairness, etc., in order to transform themselves into likeable personalities who can inspire and influence people for changing their attitude. The SICOs must be trustworthy, i.e. people in whom villagers have confidence and trust.

— The SICOs must be taught, in line, to build up their forum with the norms, rules, regulations, which they need to follow, but the underlying essence would be trust. Without mutual trust between the SICOs and other groups of people no organisational framework will run effectively.

— They have to form a plan of action with targets, goals and objectives and schedule of action, which must be translated into reality in the stipulated time period.

— The final message is that within and after the stipulated time frame, results must be measured.

Steps taken by a Cohesive Group Activated by SICO

Once a SICOs is identified (and also trained), a cohesive group may be formed. Such a group will next set its own norms. It will—

(i) Set a common goal.
(ii) Set the membership criteria.
(iii) Restructure the hierarchy pattern.
(iv) Set fixed date, place for meetings as if on a ritual basis.
(v) Set the rules and regulations.
(vi) Raise some fund through own contribution.
(vii) Keep accounts and maintain transparency.
(viii) Keep the record of resolutions of each meeting.
(ix) Set fixed criteria for reward and punishment (may not be in cash always).
(x) Set a fixed symbol/name for the group.
(xi) Organize cultural programmes in line with their own interest as well as that of the people they have to deal with.

Once a group is formed, its members would be trained for different activities. On the basis of their response to the training the bond between the members would be strengthened.

Decentralization and Activated Community Organization

West Bengal Government seeks to restructure its assistance to the health sector in the State with a view to improving efficiency, increasing public accountability regarding preventive health care service provision, and building the foundation for a more transparent and sustainable Public Health System. The Government has taken a bold step to decentralize primary health care in the hands of the community through the Panchayat functionaries. The local Gram Panchayat Pradhan has been assigned the responsibility to supervise the health centres and now he is accountable for improvement of the primary health care services in collaboration with the health officials and the village community. This is in the line of Community Managed Health System. Such experimentation has encouraging results from North 24 Parganas district of West Bengal.

To assess the impact of the programme and plan of action in accordance with the integrated effort as delineated above, a survey was undertaken in the villages of the Gram Panchayats of the Bagdah Block, viz., Helencha, Sindrani, Bagdah, Boyra, Asaru and Ranghat. These Gram Panchayats constitute two-thirds of all the Gram Panchayats in Bagdah block. The results show that all the voluntarily organized self-help groups in the villages under these Panchayats have been engaged in activities on education *(Siksha)* and savings *(Sanchay)* while they seek to tackle the problem of health *(Swasthya)*. To take one or two examples, Bainchidanga Shantikam Samity has conducted a survey on pregnant mothers and children for immunisation and then taken steps for immunisation of the children and mothers. It has also successfully launched a programme for awareness generation of the villagers regarding AIDS. Simultaneously, it has taken literacy programmes for the adults and sought to ensure readmission of school dropouts. However, the members of the group have come to face the problem of lack of people's interest in literacy programme. And, they feel that to ensure better performance, the number of SICO-led groups needs to be increased.

The villagers themselves have decided on the future plan, one main feature of which is how to make the people aware of the need for greater participation in the programme. They themselves have thought of the procedure to be followed in implementing this future plan. It is twofold: (a) the group will sit with villagers for solution of the problems regarding health and education and along with these, (b) the solution to the problem of developing the habit of savings in the village which will be a base for future income generation and thus creating confidence in the people.

Similarly, Swechcha Sevika Bahini (SSB) of Sindrani Gram Panchayat has to its credit of (i) Formation of a group of 50 women, (ii) Survey on mothers and children, (iii) Promotion of literacy of 20 adults, (iv) Generation of small savings of Rs. 3000, and (v) Immunisation of 20 mothers. But, the villagers working in the SSB are not at all complacent. Their self-assessment suggests (i) lack of sufficient awareness of the villagers regarding the immunisation of mothers and children and (ii) poor economic condition of the villagers and their inability to save. The village group itself has fixed the future plan. It relates to (i) simultaneous improvement of savings, health and education and (ii) encouragement to the villagers so that they become involved in enterprises in livestock farming and bidi-making. The procedure to be followed as per the villagers is to motivate the villagers by SICO-led groups.

Conclusion

The role and importance of community involvement at the grassroots level in development programmes is a broadly accepted notion amongst the policy makers, administrators as well as NGOs. The authors' experience at Bagdah suggests, that spontaneity in community participation in such programmes is a necessary but not a sufficient condition for the success of development projects/programmes. What is equally important is the appreciation of the integrated and dynamic nature of the process of development. There is no final static milestone or terminal point of development whatever may be the level of its realisation. In practical life basic problems like *Swasthya* (Health), *Siksha* (Education) and *Sanchaya* (Accumulation of resources or creation of a resource base) are closely interrelated. Solution of anyone of them is contingent on the solution of the others as well. In other words, community's capacity building in solving anyone of these problems implies generation of its capacity in tackling other related problems and community's success in one field leads to success in other fields as well. Active involvement of the villagers in development programmes will be based on their spontaneity and willingness, which is to be carefully nurtured through the SICOs as also on their systematic capacity building. Capacity building of panchayat functionaries and officials and people's empowerment are two integral aspects for the ongoing process of decentralization through which individuals, groups, organizations and societies can enhance their ability to identify and meet development challenges in a sustainable way.

Acknowledgements

The authors express their gratitude to CMOH of 24 Parganas (North) district and BMOH, BDO, Sabhapati and Pradhans of Bagdah Block of 24 Parganas (North) district for their helpful support. Special thanks are due to the Sabhadhipati of 24 Parganas (North) for her encouragement. The authors could not have fulfilled their commitment without the encouragement of the Sabhadhipati of 24 Parganas (North). They are extremely indebted to Professor Swapan Kumar Bhattacharyya who edited this paper with scholarly input. They acknowledge the help received from the villagers of Bagdah, Asaru, Kuladharpur, Helencha 1 No. Colony, Baichidanga, Mandapghata and other villages of Bagdah Block of West Bengal. Thanks are also due to West Bengal Health Department for providing continuous opportunity to the authors for conducting studies and making the necessary interventions.

REFERENCES

Coleman, James (1990): *Foundations of Social Theory,* Harvard University Press, Cambridge Massachusetts.

Fässler, Olivia M. (2003): *Handing Over to Local People,* published by InfoAgrar, Zollikofen.

Haq, Ul Mahbub (2002): *Human Development Report 2002,* published by UNDP.

Hesselbein, Frances (1998): *Journey to Transformation, Leader to Leader, No. 7 Winter 1998,* a publication of the Drucker Foundation and Jossey-Bass.

MacIver, R.M. and Page, Charles H. (1974): *Society—An Introductory Analysis.* Macmillan India Limited.

Putnam, Robert (1993): *Making Democracy Work: Civic Traditions in Modern Italy,* Princeton University Press.

Roy, S.B., (1992): Bilateral Matching Institutions, *Journal of Indian Anthropological Society,* Calcutta.

Roy, S.B., Mukhopadhyay, D., Das Subrata (2001): Strengthening Institutions in Joint Forest Management: Systemic Approach to Forest Conservation; *Journal of Social Science.*

Roy, S.B., Mukhopadhyay, Damayanti, Mukherjee, Raktima and Prashant (1999): 'Human Resource Development for Quality Assurance in Health Service', Paper Presented at Human Resources for Development: People and Performance Conference, University of Manchester, 28-30 June 1999.

7

THE GRAMEEN BANK
Interactive Sessions with the Stakeholders

TAPONEEL MUKHERJEE and SOURAV ROY

Introduction

The Grameen Bank is a major success story of viability of the rural poor as takers of micro credit. The Grameen Bank model is well known and is being replicated in many countries across the world. The present study is based on interactive sessions with different stakeholders of the Grameen Bank in Sadipur. One main objective of the present study was to have a first hand information regarding the working of the Grameen Bank as a source for micro finance for its members in establishing productive activities such as business units or small scale industries. Some other objectives of the present study were to assess its method of functioning, the process of attracting new members and the effectiveness of the bank's micro credit.

The Branch: Functioning and Benefits Accrued

The Sadipur branch of the Grameen Bank in Bangladesh was taken up as case study to look into the above objectives. The Grameen Bank holds meetings called "kendro sabha" at central locations within the jurisdiction of the branch. The centre discusses the loan distribution and recovery mechanism. It emerged that loans as high as 50,000 Bangladeshi taka were being loaned out to individual members who would repay it installments of 2000 taka weekly.

It was found out that the same branch and in general all branches of the bank had to face initial resistance from the local people who did not want to become members of the bank, nor obtain loan despite their poor living standards. The staff of the bank had shown exemplary patience in dealing with the local people to convince them to take loan for their own betterment whereby they could use the loan to set up small business, earn income to improve quality of life and repay loans. While interacting with the members a general sense of confidence was noticed amongst them, which comes from a sense of well-being. Members were found to be very keen to repay their earlier loan and take new loans. It was easily visible that the local people had gained confidence in themselves and the bank and were using the available loan for income generating activities. Women constituted a major proportion of the members. The ability of the members to repay amounts as high as 2000 taka weekly indicated improved status of the members availing such loans from the bank. Overall, the members seemed to be really grateful to the Bank for the contribution it had made towards the betterment of their lives.

Visit to other branches of the bank also revealed many success stories. Discussion held with the member beneficiaries have been detailed later.

Opinion of the Non-Members

In addition to the beneficiaries, contacts were made with local people who were not members of the bank in order to have their opinion regarding the functioning of the bank. A few people were not aware of the functioning of the bank as such while some had hazy idea. However, the head of the local school and other faculty members of the Panchomighat Primary and High School were selected for obtaining the required information. They were aware of the bank and knew about the nature of work being done by the bank in the area and in the country in general.

Opinion of the Bank Manager

The branch manager of Sadipur Grameen Bank has been associated with the bank for nineteen years and given his practical experience and rapport amongst the villagers, his words carry a lot of weight. It was observed that he commanded a lot of respect from his colleagues as well as the member fraternity of the branch. He was quite forthcoming and frank in his views. Below are given a few excerpts on his observations.

On Constraints Faced by the Bank

As mentioned by the branch manager, the bank faced general skepticism of rural people during the initial operations. The people were reluctant to accept what they termed as '*christian money*' due to their preconceived notion that the loans were made out of foreign funds. They were not used to strangers offering them money and help which made them suspicious. Also, due to a variety of reasons, the women of the family were not encouraged to venture out of their household activity spheres. The Grameen Bank had always given special importance to women and tried to make them members instead of menas it felt that this would be more beneficial for the rural families. The men already had jobs of some nature and so, were not in a position to provide adequate time or attention to new venture/s based on loans from the bank. Thus, the women by virtue of having more time to devote would make greater contribution to the family income. Moreover, an improvement in the social status of the women was also an added benefit of their becoming an earning member of the family.

The Grameen Bank did not have an easy task to perform. The above arguments in favour of women were important instruments in the process of convincing people about the viability of the Grameen Bank project. In the beginning, women staff members from the bank were sent to the rural areas to motivate people as they could speak directly to the women. Even if they could motivate a few women to enter the Grameen Bank project, they considered it to be enough.

On the present position of the Sadipur branch

The branch manager was in charge of the Sadipur branch for over 3 years. The total number of '*kendro*' (centres) under this branch were 70 while the total number of members were approximately 2500. The major purposes for which the loan were taken from this branch include:

- bamboo work—Burnagar kendro
- '*gamcha*' making—Panchomighat kendro
- fish farming—Jowardi, Fatehpur, Kumarchar and other centres
- jamdani sarees.

Also, 70 per cent of the members were now above the poverty line satisfying the ten indicators of poverty alleviation. This had been achieved gradually after utilizing the loan taken from this branch.

On the future vision for the branch

The manager mentioned that this branch of the Grameen bank aims to ensure that all sixteen decisions taken by the Grameen Bank [detailed later] are implemented among the member fraternity of the branch as well as to see that all of them are brought above the poverty line through utilization of loans taken from the branch. A major target would be to attain the 5 star status for the branch within the next two years. Right now, the branch has 2 stars—for being profitable and having no defaulters. They are yet to achieve stars for *gabamukti* (financial independence), *doridromukti* (all members above poverty line) and *shikkhamukti* (children of all members are educated). The concerned are working fast towards getting the first by the year-end through an increase in the savings base of the branch.

Success Stories

Case studies of two women who had utilized their loans to attain better livelihood are narrated below. The authors visited their homes and place of work and after discussion with the women individually they had the following to narrate.

Case I : "I am proud of my success !"-The Story of Moni Rani

Moni Rani has been a member of the Grameen Bank for the past 15 years. Her story is incredible in the way she has been able to change her life. She recounts that before she had taken the loan, life was very hard for sustaining her family. Her husband, Dulal Chandra Dhar, was a daily labourer in Dhaka while she lived with her son and three daughters in the village. Her first loan amount was Tk. 2500, which has now increased to Tk. 30,000. Initially, she started a business in *zari* work, which she had learnt from her father. She made costumes for the mobile *jatra* parties and earned a decent income. Within a span of 4 loan cycles, she says, their life improved enough to allow her family to think of alternative means of [higher] income. Dulal had, meanwhile, left his job and come back to stay with them. His family had been shell craftsmen for generations and this is exactly what they decided to do. Dulal mentioned that he was confident that they would do well as they had the requisite expertise to back them. They pooled in all their savings and took another loan to raise an amount to one lakh taka with which they bought 3 motors and other supplies to start their business. Today they have a flourishing business with their supplies coming from Madras, India. They even have artisans working for them who design the shell items.

The house where Moni Rani stays today is a big, well-made dwelling with a large courtyard. As she herself confesses, it is a sea change from her previous rundown shack, which was not fit even for animals. It was most interesting to see that she had built a large temple in her courtyard and organised an annual puja, bearing the entire cost. One feels that Moni

Rani's family is in many ways the ideal Grameen member family Dulal happily informed that all their children were married but there was no dowry involved in the marriages—a rarity even in today's age. As the authors were about to leave, Moni Rani stood on her doorstep and with a smile said, "please don't forget to mention that I am very proud of our success".

Case II: Amela: The Story of a Brave Woman

Amela's family consisted of, in her own words, 2 sons, 2 daughters, her husband, herself, hunger and sorrow. Such was their plight that there were times when the entire family survived on a single bowl of rice. Such conditions forced her to take a loan from the Grameen Bank, forming a group of her own. She initially took a loan of Tk. 3000, using it to purchase a rickshaw, which was her idea. Her husband pulled the rickshaw and also ran a small repair shop outside their house. Amela said, "By Allah's grace, our efforts bore fruit. We were able to take further loans and expand our horizons. It was a great change from the earlier days of struggle. We now have 3 square meals a day, some savings and could even think of acquiring more property. I had never imagined that I would have a life like this."

She managed to buy 8 rickshaws within 7 cycles of the loan graduating from there on to a baby taxi which was run by her younger son, Masood. She had acquired a large *pucca* house where she lived, another house about 3 km away and some land in the neighbouring area. Her elder son, Mohsin, ran a tyre and treading shop while her younger son operated a driving school. She had rented out 6 rickshaws, 2 baby taxis and 3 taxis. With supreme confidence, she informed the authors that in the near future she would buy a micro and, believe it or not, a bus.

All her children were matriculate and her sons were very proficient in soccer as the numerous trophies won and displayed in their home. Every family member contributed to family income and they seemed to be a satisfied lot of people. Mohsin and Masood even had their personal motorbikes that they were extremely proud of.

Over a cup of tea, Amela told the authors that the Grameen Bank has been a great help to the poor of the area and she was a great believer in the Grameen philosophy. On being told that her's was a remarkable story, she said it was all Allah's blessings.

Evaluation of the Grameen Bank

The performance of Sadipur branch of the Grameen Bank was done by mapping the past and present. Mapping is a method that can be applied in analyzing the changes that have swept a given area during a period of time. The method of mapping helps construct comparative pictures of a locality over time. It helps to capture the changes in infrastructure, standards of living and the socio-economic condition of the people of the area concerned. The effectiveness of this method, hinges on a lot of things like the knowledge of the village analyst (in this case, the school principal), his or her experience and most importantly, the ability to put down the knowledge on ground or paper. If done properly, it can give a lot of information about the changes in agricultural patterns, construction of new buildings as well as new social amenities available to the people including schools, hospitals, dispensaries, places of worship, places of entertainment and new markets.

Analyzing a map helps to yield information as to how the local people were affected by major changes in that area. The effects, positive or negative, are amply illustrated. It is especially useful in clearly specifying which institutions or individuals were responsible for those very changes as depicted by a map, which in turn helps to analyze these changes even better.

In an effort to observe the changes that have been brought about in the area in the recent past, the principal of Ponchomighat Primary and High School, an established local educational institution, constructed two maps of the area—the first depicting the area as it was twenty years ago and the second depicting the area as it is in the present times. The local school principal was requested to be the village analyst for the mapping as he was a resident of that area since his childhood and had vivid recollections about the area as it was several years ago. He drew two maps showing "before" and "after" picture of that locality.

Discussion on the Generated Maps

The maps showed the road leading from the Nayapur Bazaar to the Ponchomighat High and Primary Schools is situated next to the Brahmaputra river. This road constituted the 'lifeline' of the locality. This was made the reference point in the maps. To begin with, two decades ago, the Nayapur Bazaar was practically non-existent with the area being covered by dense vegetation. It had only a couple of small shops housed in temporary shacks and selling items required for daily use. The same could be said about the Ponchomighat Bazaar as even this market consisted of a few shacks that sold refreshments to the boatmen who came from across the river. Railway tracks used to stretch right up to Narsinghi in place of the road adjoining the Nayapur Bazaar. The 'lifeline' road of the locality of Sadipur was then nothing but a mere *kutcha* mud path weaving its way through considerable overgrowth. There were no rickshaws, buses or any other means of transport barring the sporadic railway service. Along the main road, there was nothing except a few huts but even they were few and far between. The overall description of the layout and situation of the locality seemed to suggest with a fair degree of certainty that levels of poverty were considerably high. The lives of the people did not seem to be easy at all.

The second map depicting the changes in the area over the last twenty years showed remarkable changes. The main road from Nayapur to Ponchomighat had been converted to a wide pitch road on which rickshaws and buses plied throughout the day. The buses were a very recent development with the services beginning on 11th March, 2002. It was a convenient service that had benefited the local people immensely with the gap between the two consecutive buses being less than 10 minutes. The Nayapur Bazaar had expanded to become a full-fledged market with all kinds of shops, which indicated the entrepreneurial abilities of the local residents who ran the business. The railway lines mentioned earlier, however, had been removed completely and a road now extended right from Madanganj till Narsinghi. A mosque had been built adjacent to the Nayapur bazaar. Also, along the main road, a madrasa and a primary school had been established. One of the more important developments in the area was the establishment of a *shasthyo kendro* (health centre) about 2.5 km from the market.

Situated right opposite the medical centre was the Sadipur branch of the Grameen Bank. The branch was housed in a permanent two-storied building and was a great improvement from the times when it did not even have a room of its own. The Ponchomighat bazaar served as a bus terminus and consequently had undergone a sea change from its earlier *avataar.* It was now a bustling market, full of activity throughout the day. It was spread over a large area and had a large number of shops. The Ponchomighat High and Primary Schools had also expanded and now had a proper campus consisting of four buildings and two separate playgrounds. Along the main road, a number of small shops had sprung up which were, in most cases, an extension of the house of the owner. The dwellings of a majority of the local residents had also undergone considerable change from being thatched huts with mud walls to proper houses with tin roofs. As conversations with several people revealed, earlier there were approximately one tap per thirty households while today each household had one tap each, a fair indicator of the development that the area has witnessed. The advent of electricity was yet another major step in the series of developments.

If the contribution of the Grameen Bank or to be specific, the operation of the Sadipur branch of the Grameen Bank, towards the development witnessed by the area has to be evaluated then the results will not be surprising in anyway. The branch has about 2500 members whom they have trained and prepared as per the rules of the bank. The bank has helped in the development of the area through the services rendered to these every members. The people who initially had the courage or the ability to join the Grameen Bank had managed, with exceptions being negligible, to achieve a certain degree of success in their endeavour. Within a few loan cycles, as is proved in the case studies of Moni Rani and Amela mentioned earlier, they graduated from the bottommost rung of poverty to a decent standard of living where they could manage their lives well. Their hard work had paid off. They could now afford to acquire some property, build proper houses with tin roofs, save some money for the future and several small 'luxuries' which they could only dream of earlier. These people could then influence several others around them to try and emulate their achievement, in the process awakening a desire to lead a better life than their existing one. The desire to improve their personal lives played a vital role in encouraging a pro development bent of mind among the local residents. This was, undoubtedly, a catalyst in the process of development as it made the locals want the development of the area. This was evident in the manner in which all the members mentioned about the way the area has seen so much change in the last 2 decades.

The villagers were poor, landless and assetless being completely at the mercy of the moneylenders before the intervention of the Grameen Bank. Poverty and the lack of funds meant that they could not afford to send their children to school. The overall level of education remained fairly low. Borrowing money from the local money-lenders further compounded their problems since the high rate of interest left little profit for the villagers. A lack of funds also meant that they did not have proper houses and lived in unhygienic conditions with a low level of sanitation.

It was only after the introduction of the system of micro credit through the Grameen Bank, that the entire scenario witnessed a change. With credit available to the villagers at moderate rates, they felt free to invest the money in profitable ventures. Increased availability of resources for the villagers meant that the risk taking capacity of the people had increased. As the income from the activities they indulged in increased over time, the socio-economic conditions of the people witnessed dramatic improvements. With more resources available, they managed to free themselves from the clutches of the traditional moneylenders. They were able to construct new *pucca* houses as well as toilets. This reduced the occurrence of diseases since sanitation conditions improved drastically. With an increase in resources, more and more people were willing to send their children to school. This increased the level of education, a good sign for the future generations. With income generating activities increasing, the loan taking capacity also increased. The people borrowed and invested larger amounts of money, thereby, increasing profits as well as improving socio-economic conditions further.

The Support System Diagram

Every successful scheme or project has some underlying support system, integral to the functioning of the scheme itself, which is depicted by the support systems diagram. It helps in understanding the effectiveness of the constituents of the system, its strong points, problematic areas and constraints. It is an effective visual aid which provides a tangible basis to the analysis, bringing forth the main points for scrutiny. In the diagram given below, the elementary support system of a member of the Grameen Bank has been illustrated.

The systems diagram depicts the underlying support system of the villager or the member of the Grameen Bank. The Grameen Bank can be called the input trader as it introduces money (through its system of micro credit) and seeds into the system, i.e. daily life of its member. One can correctly assume it to be the source of information, credit and skills, which makes the Grameen Bank an important ingredient of the support system. The school is also quite a necessary component as it helps educate the children of the members. This in turn results in a better future for them and reduces the chances of coming generations wallowing in poverty.

Hospitals and other similar health centres have been highly beneficial for the members. The occurrence of diseases has been reduced and their health standard has improved considerably. Another advantage of the improved health situation is a reduction in unnecessary expenditure that has to be incurred when a member of the household falls prey to some disease. Earlier, they would have to devote valuable resources to cure the person but the chances of such an occurrence were now reduced to lower levels.

Probably, the most important components of the entire support system were the large markets where the members could sell their produce and participate in transactions. Their presence had led to increase in financial as well as commercial security. People were able to sell and buy goods in the markets leading to an increase in economic activity, which, in turn, resulted in an increase in the income of those concerned. The *paikar* (wholesale trader) is also an indispensable instrument in the market activities of the members. Often, it is observed that the paikars visit the doorsteps of the members to purchase their goods. They act as the vital link between the market and the members, in the absence of which the latter may not be able to sell their goods properly.

Finally, the one factor, which has the potential to be a great support system for the members, is the spirit of brotherhood and community participation in all affairs. In fact, this proved to be the case in several areas where the Grameen Bank functioned. Villagers helped each other in times of crisis and need which bailed many a person out of trouble. The Grameen Bank fostered this spirit through its rule of formation of groups entrusted with the collective responsibility of managing their finances acquired through the loans. This was shown by the fact that inability of one member to pay a weekly installment made the remaining members of the group responsible to pay the installment amount.

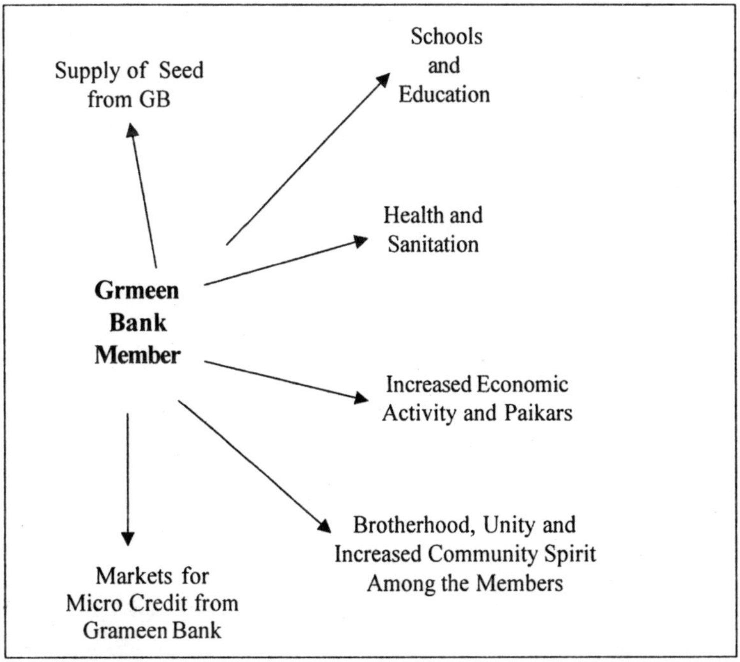

Concluding Remarks

The story of Sadipur branch shows how a practical amalgamation of vision, planning, hard work, determination along with the bank support could get an organized group of women to become high achievers and overcome the vicious cycle of poverty in the process.

Acknowledgements

The authors express their gratitude to Mrs. Nurjehan Begum, General Manager and Mr. H.A. Shah Nawaz, Deputy General Manager, of the Grameen Bank and the branch manager of Sadipur branch. They also acknowledge with gratitude the help rendered by Mr. Fazley Rabbi, Principal Officer and the staff of the Sadipur branch of the Grameen Bank.

8

PRA IN LIVELIHOODS AND BIO-DIVERSITY CONSERVATION

China

NEELA MUKHERJEE

The chapter describes exercises in participatory appraisal in three villages in a wetland in China and attempts at drawing policy implication based on the findings. The topic of biodiversity conservation in wetlands and sustainable livelihoods of local communities has attracted considerable attention in recent years. This is in view of the fact that in many Asian countries including China, wetlands constitute habitats not only for rare species of plants, animals and birds and breeding areas for migratory birds but also extend into man-made habitats of sociological world. For this reason the biological world can no longer be looked upon as an isolated and exclusive world of biodiversity conservation. It has dual functions to perform. Though its biological functions for conservation of biodiversity is of supreme importance the sociological functions of wetlands in terms of providing habitat and livelihood opportunities to the local communities is assuming considerable significance in recent years.

Though the biological world provides habitat to different types of biodiversity it is also the habitat for the local people residing in and around such areas. The local communities have stake/s in the biological world, their lives and livelihoods being intrinsically connected with the local natural resources. The earlier paradigm on conservation of biodiversity was based on a single track of biodiversity conservation and the strategy and practice was geared towards such exclusive objective. Such a strategy/

practice has gradually become outdated given the high costs and often risks involved in a single-track objective of biodiversity conservation. On the level of paradigm shift, local communities have been recognised as major stakeholders in wetland conservation and hence their perspectives have become important to reckon with (Ghimire & Pimbert, 1997). Eco-tourism is emerging as one major route to sustainable livelihood options for the local communities residing in and around wetlands. The present paper based on a case study from China draws lessons in biodiversity conservation in wetlands, eco-tourism and sustainability issues in local livelihoods.

Issues in Eco-Tourism

Though many Asian countries including China would like to develop eco-tourism activities in huge areas covered with natural wetlands they are faced with at least two major issues in many of such wetland areas. One issue is how to develop and manage the 'know-how' for eco-tourism without posing threat to the bio-diversity in the wetlands. The other issue is how to integrate aspects of eco-tourism with the biological and the sociological worlds as harmoniously as possible. It is well known that natural wetlands are one of the most threatened eco-systems in many Asian countries including China. Hence the challenge is of finding ways for preserving the basic functioning of eco-systems of wetlands in terms of water storage, climate control and bio-diversity preservation and at the same time utilising such resource base for supporting eco-tourism-related activities and other feasible livelihood options.

Eco-tourism activities have significant implications for the local communities residing in and around such wetlands. With human pressures all around wetlands preservation is also a question of providing sustainable livelihoods to local communities where eco-tourism activities can provide viable options for community involvement for "sourcing" their livelihoods and community care for bio-diversity preservation.

The present paper addresses issues in eco-tourism based on local community participation in wetland management. The objective is to draw policy implications for local community participation in wetlands and management of eco-tourism activities consistent with the principles of sustainable wetland management and at the same time creating options for sustainable livelihoods. This is significant in view of the fact that the present understanding amongst many wetland policy-makers, managers and tour operators about the complexities of wetlands as a social problem embedded within the biological world is abysmally low.

It is not always easy to understand and appreciate eco-tourism, which is aptly described below.

"Ecotourism operators" and "free independent travelers" each share a commitment to tread lightly on the land and culture, and support the local economy at their destination. Ecotourism is not defined by the distance travelled, but rather how it is accomplished and what is experienced." (by Ron Mader, Webhost/Planeta.com)

The three basic challenges generally faced in this area relate to

- Bio-diversity conservation,
- Promotion of community development, and
- Management of eco-tourism as a viable alternative.

Case Study from one National Nature Reserve in China[1] illustrates the interface between the biological and sociological worlds of the Nature Reserves and the problems and opportunities of eco-tourism as an option for alternative livelihoods. The Nature Reserve is already engaged in eco-tourism to a limited extent, for tourists visiting the Nature Reserve.

Methodology for Field Research

The case study as described in this paper is based on PRA, its principles being listening and learning through participatory interactions and learning progressively; offsetting biases, which generally accompany a 'rushed' appraisal by professionals for quick results. Such biases relate to roadside bias, seasonal bias, influential people's bias, professional bias and gender bias. PRA involves learning from diverse conditions and different actors. The process of cross-checking is also important as a principle for minimising errors and omissions. In order to minimise cost and time, the principle of optimal ignorance is a handy principle. Some selected participatory methods applied during field study are described below along with illustrations.

Participatory mapping involves spatial drawing of any area, drawn on ground, paper or on other medium by local people to show and explain their locality and other related areas, such as residential areas, forests, fields etc. Participatory mapping can include a range of items like households, school, office, infrastructure, crops, livestock, farm size, water bodies, field, forest, trees, road, facilities, common property resources, literacy, disease etc. depending on the theme/themes under discussion.

Semi-structured interview is a participatory method based more on open-ended and probing questions and hence, has a great deal of flexibility.

In semi-structured interviews, open-ended questions lead to different kinds of responses based on which further questions are designed and asked. A sequence of open-ended questions help in conducting in-depth probing of issues and their cause-effect relationship (Mukherjee, 1995).

Problem prioritisation and solutions based on ranking and scoring reveal priorities and preferences. They provide opportunities to local people to physically rank and re-rank selected items or preferences or benefits/costs and explain their reasons for a set of given ranking.

Joint walk is based on 'seeing-is-believing' and relates to learning from local communities through undertaking joint walks with them. Such walks with communities help in observing different aspects of a selected area/s in a locality, which require on-site observation and the opportunity for detailed discussions with community members.

Poverty grouping is a method of grouping of households on the basis of local indicators of poverty such as ownership of land, assets, food availability, size of family and other local measures. Different criteria can be used for poverty grouping based on local people's perceptions.

Institutional diagramming is a visual method to represent the role of individuals/institutions and the degree of their importance in decision-making. In such diagrams circle/s of different size represent individual/s and/or institution/s, whose size shows its degree of importance in local decision-making and the over-lapping of circles indicate over-lapping in decision-making.

Time line is a participatory method for tracing local changes in different variables over time such as food patterns, wages, days of work, kind of work, survival strategies, changes in vegetation, farming practices, livelihoods, quality of life etc.

In *seasonal diagramming* the local people prepare seasonal calendars using local materials either on the ground or on paper, of various socio-economic and physical phenomena such as seasonal wages received, food consumed, prices, crops grown, rainfall patterns, sickness and others.

Case Study from China

Longxi-Hongkou National Nature Reserve, Sichuan, China

The following is a case study based on a wetland in China, which is a National Nature Reserve. The name of the Reserve is Longxi-Hongkou National Nature Reserve in the Sichuan Province of China. The study is based on the methodology of PRA (Participatory Rural Appraisal) applied extensively for gaining local community insights and perspectives based on their knowledge and experience. Based on the case study selected lessons have been drawn for national and global policy-making and practice. Drawing lessons from the case study, the paper points towards the need for integrating wetland functions, eco-tourism and sustainable livelihoods for which capacity building at the local and other levels is a critical factor.

The Longxi-Hongkou National Nature Reserve is located in the Sichuan Province of China at the North-West end of the Dujiangyan city in Chengdu at a distance of 66 km. The Reserve has an area of 364 square km and a population size of 6120 and is covered by cell phone, optical fibre cable and telephone. The average altitude here is 1500 metre above sea-level, with its peak altitude at 4582 metre. There are 2500 kinds of rare plants such as the bove free, the Lianxinng, the beach, the Chinese Larch and the Xualian. Amongst the 100 mammals and 250 types of birds, 25 types of animals are under national law protection such as giant panda, golden monkey, the takin, the lesser panda, the giant salamander and the golden pheasant. The Reserve has gullies, water, waterfall, brooks and rocks making up its landscape. The tourists are attracted by the "spring flowers, cool summer resorts, autumn's falling leaves and winter snow scenes" and the hospitality of this village land. In order to attract hotel industry, the promotional material on the Nature Reserve states that it provides an ideal location for developing villas, vacation resorts and hi-tech farming.

A total of three villages were visited in the Longxi-Hongkou National Nature Reserve between November and December 2001 for holding interactive sessions with members from the local communities. The objective was to learn about village life, local livelihoods and opportunities from the villagers' perspective with the help of PRA methods. The villages covered were the following:

- Village Shengqi,
- Village Hongshe, and
- Village Gao Yuan.

The three villages gave different glimpses of the huge Nature Reserve amidst high mountains. While coming from Sichuan those villages near-by were cultivating crops and were inhabited mostly by Tibetans. Towards the middle of the Nature Reserve near its entrance a high level of construction activities were noticed in the villages mainly for tourism purposes. It was here that the tourists came and stayed. There was a bridge connecting the road and the Nature Reserve and the river flowing underneath was clearly polluted by construction materials etc. Many springs could be noticed on the way. Going further down on the main road those villages could be seen where there were more trees and little or no farmlands. Interacting in the three villages gave insights into three different parts of the Nature Reserve and three different perspectives of local communities.

The PRA sessions with the villagers threw up interesting results. In the Longxi-Hongkou National Nature Reserve the local communities were actively engaged in eco-development. Some of them were participating not only as hosts for tourists but were also involved in planting trees and reducing farmlands. The local communities grew radish, carrots, beans, and leafy vegetables on small patches of land in the Nature Reserve. Amongst fruit trees they mainly grew Kiwi trees for fruits. They also grew Magnolia trees to sell the bark for medicinal usage. There was a project on "reducing farmland and increasing trees" run by the Government of China in 1999 for the local communities residing in the Longxi-Hongku Nature Reserve. Under this project they received assistance for two years in terms of 100 kg of rice for 3 months in a year and were required to substitute rice crop through growing of fruit trees such as Kiwi and other creepers.

Before 1999, though many farmers started planting Kiwi trees there was no support available from the government. Whereas after 1999, under the project "reducing farmland and increasing trees" local Government provided seedling of Kiwi and financial assistance of 100 Yuan per 'Mu' (local unit where 15 Mu = 1 hectare) per year for a period of 2 years. The economics of Kiwi trees shows that one Kiwi tree yielded at least 40 kg of fruits in the season, whereas the fruit was sold at the rate of 2 Yuan per kg (approximately) (1 US Dollar is equivalent to around 8 Yuan).

Those residents growing Kiwi trees as a means of livelihood had seasonal income, which sustained them for a few months. This income was supplemented by other activities such as raising livestock. Many members of the local communities also raised livestock such as pigs and ducks. The livestock manure helped them to support Kiwi trees. For Kiwi fruit trees more than 12 pig's manure was required for 100 trees. The trees required at least 4 times manure per year. Those possessing less number of pigs took manure from those possessing more number of pigs.

Near the main entrance of the Nature Reserve, some of the local residents were engaged in tourism supporting activities. They offered places for stay to the tourists, many of whom came from Sichuan. There were different types of tourists some with high budget while others with low and medium budgets. More tourists came during the spring season. The potential of having more tourists led to construction of big buildings and other concrete structure, which were out of gear with the landscape of the Nature Reserve. This had also led to an increase in construction activities within the Nature Reserve thus leading to noise and other disturbances and also air and water pollution. With increase in vegetable and Kiwi production, the local community members were strongly in favour of replacement of the hanging wooden bridge over the river by a permanent structure. They were willing to exchange village land for construction of a permanent bridge.

A time line done by a group of villagers in village Honghsu in Longxi-Hongkou Nature Reserve showed the changes in the Nature Reserve between 1960 and 2001 as follows. As shown in Chart 8.1 the number of trees fell between 1960 and 1990 but again increased between 1990 and 2001. The size of human population in that area increased over time though such increase was relatively less during1960s as compared to that between 1980 and 2001. The size of wildlife though big in 1960 with no access road in the area, fell in 1980 due to increase in hunting activities and later registered increase between 1990 and 2001. As stated by the local people this was the impact of wildlife conservation policy of the Government as translated into practice. The area under farmland increased sharply between 1960 and 1990 but fell sharply in later years so as to become zero in 2001.

Chart 8.1: Time Line on Longxi-Hongkou National Nature Reserve

Year	Number of Trees	Size of Human Population	Size of Wildlife	Area under Farmland
1960	♣♣♣♣♣ ♣♣♣♣	♣♣♣♣	♣♣♣♣♣♣ ♣♣♣♣♣	♣♣♣♣
1980	♣♣♣♣♣	♣♣♣♣♣♣ ♣♣♣♣♣♣	♣♣♣♣♣♣	♣♣♣♣♣ ♣♣♣♣
1990	♣♣♣♣	♣♣♣♣♣♣♣ ♣♣♣♣♣♣	♣♣♣♣♣ ♣♣♣♣♣	♣♣♣♣♣♣♣ ♣♣♣♣♣♣♣
2001	♣♣♣♣♣ ♣♣♣♣♣	♣♣♣♣♣♣♣ ♣♣♣♣♣♣♣	♣♣♣♣♣♣♣♣ ♣♣♣♣♣♣♣♣	No more farm land

Note: The above time line was prepared on the ground by an elderly woman by the name of Miao Xiufen along with other villagers in her home compound. She used maize seeds as scores for showing the qualitative changes in the four aspects—trees, human population, wildlife and farmland. The symbols in the table above show the changes for each aspect/variable over time. More 'score' means higher availability while less 'score' means lower availability.

Effectiveness of the project in "reducing farmland and increasing trees"

The project "reducing farmland and increasing trees" was effective to the extent that the local communities actually reduced their farmlands though simultaneously coping with uncertainties such as diversifying and securing livelihoods other than farming. The compensation given by the Government in terms of food was for a short term and not that adequate. Hence the local communities coped with the policy of reducing farmland by diversifying their livelihoods. They planted fruit trees, medicinal plants and vegetables on the land and other patches they had. In two years time they were able to diversify their livelihoods from farming to other activities so as to adapt to the new policy.

Some villages located near the main entrance of the Nature Reserve started doing eco-tourism during seasons when tourists visit the Nature Reserve. Many villagers constructed buildings to accommodate the tourists and this partially damaged the landscape of the Reserve. Many concrete structures were not eco-friendly and did not go well with the habitat of the Nature Reserve. They stood out as sloppy buildings amidst Nature and spoiled the ambience. The tourists were provided with all the comforts by the local people practicing tourism and they could prove damaging to he ecosystems and habitat for bio-diversity all-around.

Some Lessons for Policy Making and Practice

We can draw some lessons from the above case study for policy making and practice. One point is obvious. Eco-tourism activities may not be enough to provide livelihoods to local communities throughout the year. Such activities may be seasonal activities and they are not enough activities for all those residing in such wetlands and desiring to do such activities to gain livelihoods. If wetland has to be conserved on a sustainable basis, eco-tourism is only a part of the answer. Many Nature Reserves/Park/biological worlds are relatively small in size as compared to the population living around them. Hence, in terms of sustainable livelihoods it may not be possible to create/accommodate viable livelihoods for the entire population of local communities residing in and around such areas. Much depends on the potential of Nature Reserves to create opportunities for the local communities. The carrying capacities of many Nature Reserves are limited in terms of fodder, fuelwood and other livelihood opportunities. It is important to map the backward and forward linkages of eco-tourism for involving local communities and also to explore viability of other productive activities at the local level for gaining livelihoods.

For any collaborative arrangement with local communities in wetlands it is important to identify mutual benefits and costs and negotiate on that basis. If a realistic picture of benefits and costs is not shared with the local communities then it can become a basis for future conflict. Often local communities expect considerable benefits when new interventions get initiated in Nature Reserves though projects aiming at conservation with development. Hence, it is important to have a participatory assessment of potential benefits and costs together with local communities for realistic assessment. This can be followed by having interactive sessions with local communities in a negotiating framework of 'give and take'. The local communities need to be explained the extent of benefit that can emerge from community participation in Nature Reserve management and bio-diversity conservation. The collaborative matrix can be applied for seeking collaboration with local communities for mutually supportive activities and win-win situation.

For collaborative arrangements it is relatively easy to start with "pilot" villages and then expand to include more villages. All joint activities of Nature Reserve with local communities need to have enough stakes of the local communities so as to feel interested in carrying out negotiated activities, which are mutually beneficial for both Nature Reserves and the local communities. It will be useful to closely monitor agreements on activities in the pilot villages by setting up a joint monitoring group of the local communities and the officials of the respective Nature Reserves.

Micro Credit Activities

The results from the field exercises in different villages show that the local communities face considerable shortage of credit for different activities. Micro credit activities need to be started in these villages with the help of NGOs or some suitable organization. Capacity building in Micro Credit and Savings and Credit Group Formation and Management can be undertaken at the local level by different donor agencies. Skill formation in savings/credit group formation, user-group dynamics, management of such groups, process of social mobilization etc. Such a study tour will help them to understand and appreciate the different ways in which such savings and credit groups can be formed and managed and the opportunities and ways to overcome the constraints.

Whichever model/s of savings and credit group making is adapted consultation and discussions with local communities are crucial on different aspects of such group formation and functioning. Elaborate consultation with members of the local communities in the nature Reserve is an integral part of the whole process for deciding the framework on the following. All savings and credit groups need to be based on the active involvement of the stakeholders with contribution of funds from both local community members and the Nature Reserve in question. Women groups and self-help groups of poor people can be promoted through special incentives by Nature Reserve keeping special needs of such groups in perspective. For identifying the scale of credit requirement and type of credit interactive sessions with community members are important. Some important aspects of such group formation are as follows:

(i) Types of group-based savings and credit activities;
(ii) Its constituent members;
(iii) The size of each group and powers the groups would enjoy;
(iv) The leadership criteria for groups;
(v) The policy regarding the rate of interest and usage of funds;
(vi) The policy of loans/withdrawals/frequency of group meetings etc.;
(vii) Issues regarding record-keeping and accounting practices; and
(viii) Policy regarding supervision and monitoring.

Conservation Awareness and Education

Conservation awareness in school-education could be linked with conservation in local villages around Nature Reserve. Awareness building on "plastic" re-cycling and sustainable use is important.

"Demonstration" Plots for Green/Organic Farming

"Demonstration" plots can be set up in the pilot villages of different Nature Reserves for demonstrating green/organic farming practices. This can be tied up with organizations, which run similar courses in green/organic farming.

There are clear lessons to be learnt from different Nature Reserves about sustainable use of resources and practices. For example, farmers from other National Nature Reserve in other parts of China can visit some villages of Longxi Hongkou National Nature Reserve at Sichuan Province to see for themselves how the villagers are practicing sustainable vegetable cultivation without involving chemical fertilizers and pesticides and yet getting good crop production. They can also learn about the manure-making from pig droppings and also about the practices in horticulture. Also the staff of other Nature Reserves in China can visit selected villages of Longxi Hongkou NNR to find out for themselves the lessons from the project on "reducing farmlands and increasing tree plantation", its strength and limitations, local issues and ways of improving upon collaboration with local communities.

Afforestation Activities

The Nature Reserves authority can undertake activities such as tree plantation and protection activities in collaboration with the local communities in the "pilot" villages with joint supervision and management. Mutual sharing of benefits and harvesting of trees need to be negotiated up-front.

Supporting Income Generating Activities

Different Nature Reserves can collaborate with the local communities for different income generating activities such as cow keeping, pig keeping, duck raising etc. on a mutually beneficial basis so as to treat them as 'entry' points activities for local communities to support conservation activities in and around the Nature Reserves. Such support from the Nature Reserve would also help in building channels of mutual trust and cooperation with the local communities living in and around the Nature Reserves. Again 'entry' points in "pilot" villages will help in understanding the 'nuts' and 'bolts' of managing such collaboration in practice before it is extended to other villages.

Conducting Studies in Scope for Eco-Tourism Activities

Potential of local communities in eco-tourism activities needs to be explored in depth by each of the Nature Reserve. Such eco-tourism activities can form an integral part of alternative livelihood system. Based on present tourist inflow, the type of tourist, the potential tourist inflow and other criteria, there needs to be an in-depth professional study on the eco-tourism potential and practical strategies of the Nature Reserves included under the Project. For initiating such studies, appropriate organizations can be contacted for assessing such eco-tourism potential and also for possible ways of capacity building of the local communities.

There is a balancing act for eco-tourism in wetlands. Given the threatened eco-systems of wetlands in Asia, eco-tourism needs to be managed in such a manner so that the integral values and functioning of wetlands are maintained and enriched and also such activities yield reasonable pay off at the local level. It is important to recognise the need for integrating wetland functions, eco-tourism and sustainable livelihoods for which promoting and maintaining indigenous knowledge and practices are important. Capacity building and awareness generation at local level and other levels is important. The types of capacity building for eco-tourism would depend on the type of wetlands, their status and significance, their degradation factor, local community perspectives, existing skills, existing practices, wetland policy framework and the nature of eco-tourism-related activities. With building of appropriate capacities at different levels, the three basic challenges of bio-diversity conservation, promotion of community development and sustaining eco-tourism activities can be met to a reasonable extent.

NOTE

1. See promotional material on the Hongxi Longkou National Nature Reserve, China.

REFERENCES

Cai Kui, "PRA Network and the Role of PRA Approach in Rural Development of China", Rural Development Research Center (RDRC) at Yunan Institute of Geography, Kunming, China.

Centre for integrated Agricultural Development (CIAD), (1996): "Training Course on PRA/ZOPP abd Workshop on Participatory Approach to Rural Community Integrated Development" *Report 3,* CAFIU/PLAN, Yanqing County Rural Community Integrated Development Project, CIAD, China Agricultural University, Beijing, September.

Chinese PRA Network, PRA reading materials, Guizhou PRA Network and Yunan PRA Network material on PRA in Gahai Lake (all in Chinese languange).

Claridge, Gordon and Bernard O' Callaghan, (1997): *Community Involvement in Wetland Management: Lessons from the Field*, Wetlands International.

DFID (1998): *Sustainable Rural Livelihoods What contribution can we make?* Edited by Diana Carney, Department for international Development, London, July.

Ghimire, K.B. and Michel Pimbert (ed.), (1997): *Social Change and Conservation*, Earthscan Publications, London.

Hengfang, Zou, (1998): "Participatory Methodologies in the Planning and Design of Forestry Projects", *Forestry and Society Newsletter*, November.

Metzner, Keith A. (2000): "Training Needs Analysis Report for Ruoergai Wetland", 26 December, Reference 4.4, Wetland Biodiversity Conservation and Sustainable Use in China, Project Number: CPR/98/G32.

Mission Report, (2000): "Training Needs Assessment Report for Sanjiang Plain in Heilongjiang Province, November", by Neela Mukherjee, Wetland Biodiversity Conservation and Sustainable Use in China, Project Number: CPR/98/G32.

Mukherjee, Neela (1994): *Participatory Rural Appraisal, Methodology and Applications*, Concept Publishing Company, New Delhi.

Mukherjee, Neela, (1997): *Participatory Appraisal of Natural Resources*, Concept Publishing Company, New Delhi.

Mukherjee, Neela, (2000): *Participatory Learning and Action: With 100 Field Methods*, Concept Publishing Company, New Delhi.

Robinson, Eva Cheung, (1993) "A PRA Training Experience in Kunming, China", Institute of Development Studies, Sussex.

Shen *et al.* (1996): "The Application of PRA in Chinese Rural Development Research", *Forestry and Society* (in Chinese Languange) 5 May.

Swanson Timothy, (1997): *Global Action for Biodiversity,* Earthscan Publications, London.

UNDP (1996): "UNDP's 1996 Report on Human Development in Bangladesh A Pro-Poor Agenda", Poor People's Perspectives, UNDP, Dhaka.

Wang, Caroline, Yuan Yan Ling and Feng Ming Ling, (1994): "Photovoice as a tool for Participatory Evaluation: The community's View of Process and Impact", *Journal of Contemporary Health*, 4:47-49.

Wilkes, Andreas, (1996): "Trip Report: Current Issues in China – Discussions about PRA in Kunming and Beijing", 2-9 December, 1996, Institute of Development Studies, Sussex.

WWF and Keoladeo National Park, (1996): *Participatory Management Planning for Keoladeo National Park*, WWF International, New Delhi.

Zhengmuo, Guo, (1996): "Farmer Participation in the Management and Policy-making of Forestry Projects", *Forestry and Society Newsletter,* Vol.4, No. 2, November.

9

PARTICIPATORY RESOURCE MAPPING OF VILLAGES

RUPA DASGUPTA, SWATI LAHIRI, R. SONI, ROBI DASGUPTA
and M.V.R.L. MURTHY

Introduction

Rural India is divided into blocks, which are in turn divided into villages. The size of a village varies, as does its character, which depends on the resources available in terms of manpower, skill, and natural or geographical location. There is wide variation in the level of development amongst the villages. There are several types of programmes/plans being implemented by the government and by NGOs to improve upon the living conditions of the villagers. Some development plans are in terms of infrastructure building or setting up of appropriate capital assets in the villages. For any of the above development, knowledge of the presently available facilities, resources, human resources and skill availability is essential. It is difficult to get updated first hand information regarding the above from the designated agencies in the villages for the purpose. A technique was applied for mapping the resources available in a village onto the village map by people's participation. The resources identified relate to both natural and manmade resources. The present paper describes the method adopted in detail, the resources mapped and the benefits, which can be accrued from such a mapping. A case study from a particular village has also been provided.

The Method

The basic purpose of resource mapping of a village is to enable planners to plan for the future of the village based on the available resources. It is aimed to achieve the above by people's participation. The village map was collected from the block development office. The map was divided into zones for ease of mapping and identification. One main landmark in the complete village map or a number of landmarks preferably one in a particular zone was selected and marked on the map, depending on the size of the village.

Village level meetings were held in a number of clusters and the purpose of the whole exercise was explained to the villagers. Volunteers were requested to help in mapping of resources on the map. For broad-based participation, at least one person from each household was requested and asked to participate. Such wide participation was encouraged to evince people's interest and do away with disparities. Clusters of villagers residing in a particular locality were gathered and the village level map shown. The houses were marked on the map and shown to them. The number of people in a cluster was considered appropriate so that all could see and visualize their entire locality through the participatory map. The resources, which need to be marked, were explained to them and they were asked to mark them directly on the map. Each resource was given a particular symbol. For quantification, darker shades of the same symbol were used. The darkness of the colour was directly related to the quantity. A qualitative assessment relating the quantity with the shade was explained.

The person(s) conducting the mapping maintained a list of symbols and designated shade for uniformity. The locality, whose people were participating in the meeting, were shown their locality on the map and asked to mark their house, their field and the resources on the map. All such markings were confined to that locality only whose people participated. The idea of involving more people for identification other than the key informants was a way of cross-checking, ownership and to evolve a clearer picture. All the concerned people discussed amongst themselves regarding actual location of items and probable quantity (wherever applicable) and then marked it on the map. The same map was then taken to the next adjoining locality and the same procedure followed. In this way complete mapping of the village was done and cross-checked. It was essential to maintain continuity between localities to evolve a clear picture specially for mapping resources related to infrastructure.

Resources for Mapping

Resources chosen for mapping by this particular method could be many and would vary depending on the purpose of the mapping. For a general case, the resources that could be generally mapped are categorized as follows:

- Household
- Forest area
- Agricultural area
- Natural resources
- Geographical locations
- Infrastructure
- Social establishments
- Cultural locations

Household location would include marking the household at the exact position, its nature, i.e. whether mud or cemented and an approximate size. It could also show the adjoining land around the house and the purpose for which it is used. Any tube well or well located within the premises could be marked. The house could be designated by a symbol or alphabet say "H" which could be encircled and a tube well or well marked by "t" or "w". The colour of the symbol for house could vary depending on the nature of the house for example it could be light brown for mud and dark brown for cemented house. The adjacent area of the house could correspond to the size, and the use of the area marked on it. Different options of using the adjacent areas could be thought of before and mentioned to the villagers so that they are able to designate it properly. For example, different symbols could be allocated for different use of land for instance, for agricultural purpose, domestic purpose such as for cattle shed/breeding etc. or kept vacant.

The forest area in the locality being mapped could be marked with designated symbol/s. Different colours for the symbol could be used to designate different produce of the forest. In case there is no sharp demarcation, i.e. the forest area does not produce a particular variety, different colours could highlight all the varieties produced. If possible the density of the forest area could also be depicted by using darker shades of the colour or by marking through symbols.

Similarly, the agricultural area of the locality could be symbolized and the type of produce marked on the map by using different colours. For example if the agricultural area is symbolized by "#", red colours could be used for potatoes, green for wheat, yellow for paddy, and the like.

Natural resources and geographical locations would include mountains, rivers, ponds, lakes, etc. This would vary depending on the geographical location of the village. These could be designated by different symbols for marking on the map. The area could be symbolized by area of a circle corresponding to its size. This requires a pre-determined correspondence of the size of the area to the size of the circle. In case of flowing rivers and mountain range the direction of flow could be marked.

Infrastructure, which could be mapped include roads, highways, schools, colleges, parks, market place, weekly haats, bus stand, railway station, government offices, etc. Different symbols could be used for each. Roads could be designated as tar road or mud road with different colour or shades of colour. The direction of the road could also be marked. In addition to the above, there could be some special infrastructure for a village, which needs to be marked. Efforts made to designate all the available infrastructure facilities of a village are beneficial to planning activities at a later stage.

Social and cultural locations would include community halls, places of worship, places of gathering, panchayat *bhawan* etc. Keeping in mind the social background of rural India, it could be beneficial if residential areas/locations having residents from a particular social/religious background reside are marked. This could be a significant piece of information while designing social interventions.

Utility of the Resource Map

The village resource map generated by the above type of study could be used either for identifying/mapping the following resources, which could then be used for generating database, planning and utilizing local resources. The resources include:

- Geographical locations,
- Natural resources,
- Agricultural produce,
- Forest area,
- Social and physical Infrastructure available.

A mapping of this nature would help in future planning of local resources. This would include setting up of industrial units or entrepreneurial units depending upon the quantity and quality of raw material available. Knowledge of the infrastructure available like roads, market etc. would help in designing the marketability of the produce. Geographical locations like river and facilities like dam and availability of electricity in adjoining areas would help in chalking out the feasibility of setting up units in the area. From knowledge of the skill available with the people it would be helpful in knowing the type of support and artisans that would be available locally, as any unit would require involvement of people with some specified skills. Knowledge of the social establishments would help in gauging the level of social commitment and nature of involvement of the community for social causes. For example, a community hall in the area would mean that people gather there to discuss and participate in social activities. From this it can be assessed that in future if a social gathering is required people have a place to participate; and also any decision or discussion could be initiated at such a location.

Case Study

A village Bamhani was taken up for mapping in the Tamia block of Madhya Pradesh, an essentially tribal block. The participatory map shows the infrastructure, geographical and natural resources. For ease of reference, two separate maps were drawn for natural resources and infrastructure.

Concluding Remarks

A study of this nature would help in identifying different types of resources in a village set-up. The study can be extended to a cluster of villages and eventually for the block as a whole. The advantage with this type of mapping is that it is being done with local people's participation, after discussion and in a group. It should however be borne in mind that a lot of foresight is required for this job; it requires detailed listing of the possible resources, and designating individual symbols with the correct shade of colour (for quantification). The villagers need to be briefed about the mapping exercise through village level meetings before hand so that they own the process, come up with ideas and get a feel for the whole thing. This type of mapping would finally be beneficial to government or other departments who are interested in planning, whether participatory or not for the village.

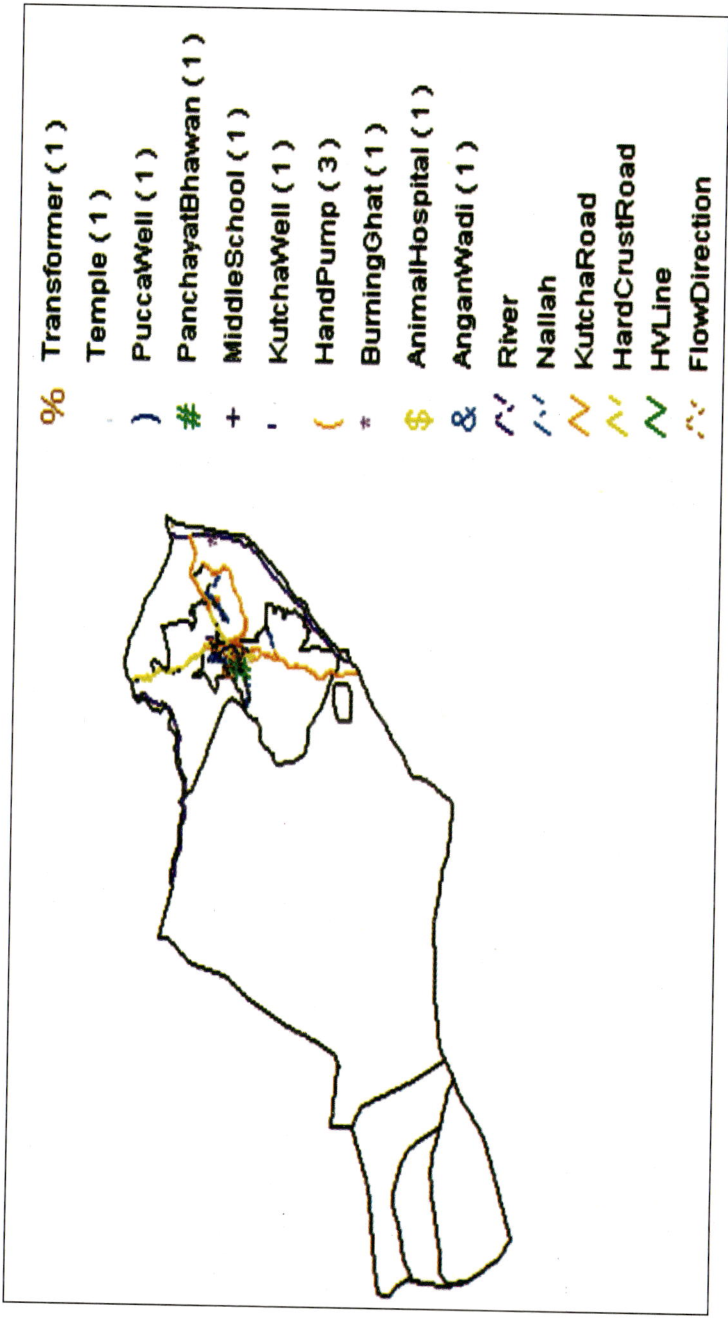

Fig. 9.1 : Transformer

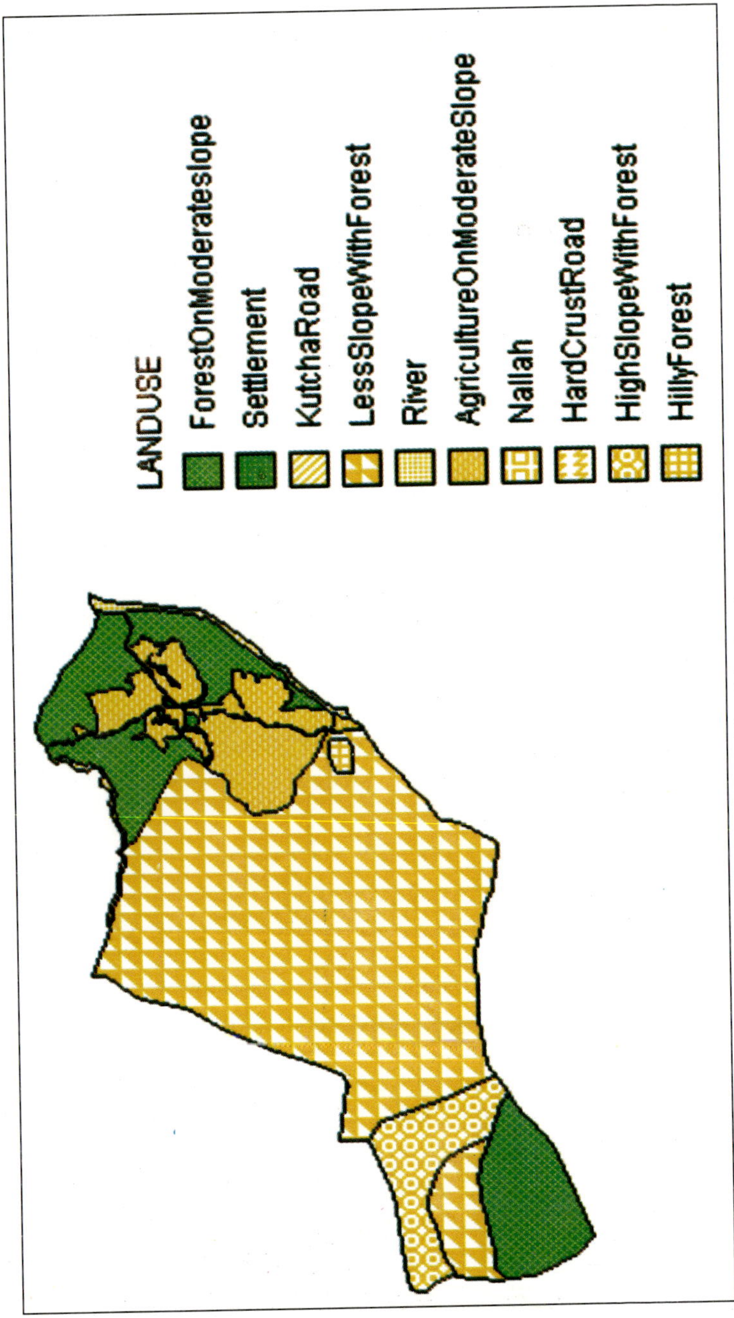

Fig. 9.2 : Landuse

Acknowledgements

The contents of the paper is an outcome of the exercise done during implementation of an UNDP-DST-GOI supported programme on "Support to Rural Technology Development and Application Centres and block level Technology Resource Centres". This programme is being implemented at the Regional Research Laboratory, Bhopal that is a constituent R&D laboratory under the Council of Scientific & Industrial Research (C.S.I.R.). The authors are thankful to the sponsor of the sub-programme for providing an opportunity to be associated with such a sub-programme.

10

UPWARD-DOWNWARD MOBILITY IN WELL-BEING

DEBABRATA BASU, DURBA BISWAS and RUPAK GOSWAMI

While writing on poverty and well-being drawing on Sen's concepts is almost taken for granted, but when we borrow his line "poverty is no less funny", presumably eclectically, at the very outset, we do feel embarrassed for at lest two reasons—firstly, the feeling of poverty in no way invokes fun (at least in part of those who experience it), and secondly, even the researchers are not able to recognize enough and measure the fun of poverty unquestionably. There are different worldviews on poverty (from the view of only the poor or only the non-poor or both), different approaches in measurement (biological approach, inequality approach, relative deprivation approach), dichotomy of conditions and feelings of poverty, and methods of measurement, from which the concerns of participatory approach for well-being measurement constitutes the main thrust of this paper. This paper is concerned with the method of well-being ranking, a widely employed method across the world and looks into the unexplored sphere of poverty dynamics. The paper searches for a befitting tool to measure it. Upward-downward mobility in well-being is such a tool, the heart of our present paper.

In the last few decades there have taken place major shifts in the economic, political, social and cultural fronts and are poised to continue in the foreseeable future. Changes are occurring both at the individual as well as agency levels. Conceptualising and measuring poverty and well-being, hence, have to conform to this changing reality. The well-being of people often changes absolutely as well as relatively over time without any intended interventions. Again, it is also borne by factual experience that different development programmes initiated by Government and voluntary organizations give impetus towards positive change. Upward and downward mobility of the people along the well-being ladder is, hence, of obvious interest to understand the result of the local, complex, diverse, and dynamic realities, interacting with the ever changing and multifaceted outside factors of influence.

Meaning of Well-being and Upward-Downward Mobility

Well-being means the experience of good qualities of life. Income or wealth is, of course, not the only factor that affects a family's well-being. Well-being and poverty are didactically interdependent. Talking about one automatically involves and takes care of another. While elaborating the concept of "deprivation trap" Chambers (1990) found that poverty usually goes hand in hand with physical weakness, vulnerability (to hunger, illness, natural disasters, exploitation, further loss of already limited recourses), powerlessness and isolation (including lack of education, services, general remoteness etc.). Well-being is just opposite to this, involving strength and versatility (of the person, the households and production strategy), patronage, authority and power, and access to both local and wider resources including education (and job opportunity) and other services.

In recent times, a lot of debate has taken place among social scientists and developmental economists regarding the meaning of well-being. Sen (1992) has distinguished between the "well-being aspect" and "agency aspect" of a person. According to him well-being refers to the needs, interests and goals, which the person wants to achieve. While doing that, the person may also try to pursue the agency's well-being. Freedom of a person for achieving her well-being is another important aspect and freedom and well-being may not always move together in the same direction. Freedom here includes both "agency freedom" and "well-being freedom" (Sen, 1992).

Dasgupta (1993) has tried to provide some indicators and suggested ways by which the well-being of a person could be measured. These are as follows:

(i) Income,
(ii) Health in terms of (a) anthropometric measures, (b) mortality indices, (c) morbidity, and
(iii) Education.

Chambers (1997) has conceptualised the "web of responsible well-being" consisting of five important concepts, each of which are closely linked together. These are presented schematically in Fig 10.1

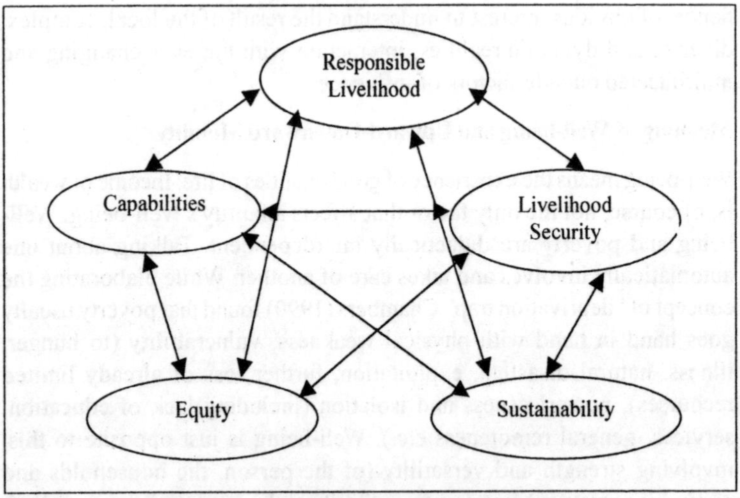

Fig. 10.1: Web of responsible well-being.

The total well-being of a family depends on four dimensions of well-being as perceived by the poor from different parts of the world. These include "material well-being" (food security and employment), "psychological well-being" (power and voice; cultural and social norms), "state provided infrastructural facilities for well-being" and lastly, "the assets of the poor" (physical capital, human capital, social capital and environmental assets) (Narayan *et al.*, 2000).

Well-being ranking is a popular and widely employed participatory learning and action (PLA) tool found effective in capturing the differences in well-being of the households of a particular area as perceived by local people. In this technique a small group of people (key informants) rank and group themselves and their peers on the basis of their criteria of well-being. But the well-being position of a household in a particular area does not remain static over time. As a result of changing realities, say as the consequence of development progammes, some households evolve to occupy better position (i.e. higher rank in the well-being ladder) and just the opposite may happen to some other households. This upward (i.e. higher rank than before) and downward (i.e. lower rank than before) movement of well-being positions of households along well-being ladder is called upward and downward mobility. "The technique can be helpful in monitoring the impact of aid distribution and development endeavours along with identifying and understanding the dynamics of local criteria of well-being and changes in wealth. Upward-downward mobility is, therefore, of immense importance in assessing the impact of a development programme".

Methodology for Upward-Downward Mobility—its Strength/Limitations

The method of present concern (upward-downward mobility) may be thought as an extension of well-being ranking adapted to assess the temporal fluctuation of peoples' well-being. Among different methods of well-being ranking 'card sorting' (Grandin, 1988) deserves advocacy for the present purpose with appropriate adaptations. This is a group exercise and the key informants of the area, where the study is to be conducted are identified to participate in the exercise. The key informants are then asked to write the names of the head of the households on the cards supplied to them. If the key informants are illiterate, then the facilitator writes the names for him/her or pictorial chart/social map may be used for this purpose. Then the key informants are asked to sort out the cards into different piles on the basis of their criteria of well-being. Each pile represents a well-being class and each card among the piles represents a well-being rank.

For assessing upward-downward mobility, the above mentioned process has to be repeated twice. In a sense it is a "before-after" research design, where the first card sorting is conducted as a benchmark and the second one after the termination of the project. But if the benchmark card sorting had not been done, "recall" method can be employed, where those earlier key informants are involved, who had witnessed the situation before the project initiation and can recall the situation vividly. This before-after well-being ranking will help to identify the families that have changed their positions along the well-being ladder by the time of the project/programme completion. Afterwards, probing is necessary to find out the reasons behind both the changed and unchanged positions of the families. The total outcome is presented in a tabular form for easier interpretation and understanding. However, this method, like others, is not a panacea in itself and has its intrinsic strengths and limitations as well. Some of them are described below.

Strengths

- It helps in identifying the number of households who have actually benefited from the assistance given by the project.
- This is an easy and less time consuming method involving local participation directed towards the identification of local indicators of well-being and also changes in the indicators over time.
- It also indicates the reasons behind the up and down movement along well-being ladder in the context of changing local reality. This helps the project planners identify where to emphasize during re-orientation of the project or during planning of new project in the same area.
- It helps to probe into the fact why some of the assisted families have improved their condition and why the others have not been able to do so.

Limitations

- The well-being ranking through card sorting functions well in groups/communities of about 50 to 150 members (Theis and Grady, 1991).
- To perform this exercise, for identifying upward-downward mobility, the informants should have in-depth information about each and every family in the community. If the number of families in the community is too large, it is not possible for the informants to know all the families. In the latter case, card sorting will be erroneous, affecting the findings regarding mobility.
- This method is of no use in the areas where there is constant in and out migration of people.
- The method does not reveal the mystery in case of relative change in one's household's well-being is the result of another household's change in the well-being position. This implies that it cannot trace the existing distributional problem within the society.

Application and Analysis

There are many interesting studies on upward-downward mobility conducted in different parts of the world. Three examples from India in the form of case studies are described below.

Upward-downward mobility in well-being is an effective method/tool to assess the well-being positions of different households in a particular area that changes with the passage of time. Though it is a complex process to get the pulse of the dynamic reality of the society, the method identifies the reasons behind intra-group and inter-group mobility

Case Study-1

The first study was conducted in the village of "Punglapur" in Birbhum district of West Bengal. Here Lutheran World Service-India, a reputed NGO, initiated a rural development programme in 1994. During the evaluation of this programme in 1997, upward-downward mobility in well-being was studied as a part of participatory evaluation process. The village was very small and consisted of only forty families. On the second day of visit to the village, the reliable local informants were identified with the help of community leaders. After a brief introduction, they were supplied with cards and asked to write the names of head of each household on each card. Then the informants were asked to sort those cards into different well-being groups based on their own perception of indicators. They divided the cards into five groups, namely, Group-A: Destitute, Group-B: Poorest, Group-C: Poor, Group-D: Moderate and Group-E: Well off (Table 10.1), and on asking they wrote the indicators for each group and also the reasons for placing a family at a particular position of a particular group on the back side of the very card.

Afterward, they were supplied with the well-being ranking done at the inception of the programme. It was shown to the informants only after they had done the post-programme ranking in order to avoid any biasness on their part. They compared these two rankings and identified the households that have changed their positions in well-being (both upward and downward). They also narrated the reasons underlying this change. Inter-group and intra-group mobility were also identified quite efficiently.

Source: Field notes of Debabrata Basu, 1997.

Case Study-2

Village "Kantamari" of South 24-Parganas district in West Bengal had a rural development programme initiated by Lutheran World Service-India since 1992. During the impact analysis of the programme through participatory evaluation in 1997, a study of upward-downward mobility in well-being was conducted. There were 311 families in the village and as a result, it required more time for the application of the tool than that of the previous case. In fact, for evaluation purpose the villagers participated in different group exercises using few PLA tools for the first few days. Therefore, it was somewhat easy to identify informants for upward-downward mobility assessment. On the fourth day, the evaluation team met the informants and asked to group each card for each household into different well-being groups (Table 10.2) on the basis of their perception of criteria. This took about three hours to complete the exercise. On the following day the team provided them the benchmark well-being ranking and asked to compare the two. They identified the families, which changed their position upward and amongst these families who participated in the programme. Further probing helped to identify the reasons behind both the changed and unchanged situations. This day's exercise took two hours to get over.

Source: Field notes of Debabrata Basu, 1997.

Case Study-3

In Chittoor district of Andhra Pradesh a watershed development programme was implemented by an NGO named Rural Education and Action for Change (REACH) in Doranakambala watershed during 1997. The programme had undergone a participatory evaluation (PE) in 2001 and as a part of this PE a study of upward-downward mobility in well-being was conducted. The watershed consisted of only 80 families.

On the first day of the study, the key informants were identified with the help of local leaders and NGO staff. Then with their consent the place, date and time were fixed for conducting the exercise. On the day of meeting, the informants were asked to categorise the families in different well-being groups through card sorting; the exercise took nearly two hours. But in this case, interestingly, the benchmark well-being ranking was not available. Thus "before-after" method was not used; rather on the following day the informants were requested to recall the situation in 1997 and on that basis they mentioned the position of their families, especially of those who had changed their position (Table 10.3). Reasons underlying upward-downward mobility and unchanged positions were also discussed. This job was completed within about three hours.

Source: Field note of P. Papoorna, 2001

with comparative ease and thus helps to have a vision of better opportunities for the people who show upward intra-group mobility to achieve inter-group upward mobility. It has often proved to be a less time consuming and easier method contributing towards the active participation of the people.

This method under discussion addresses some systematic problems that stream out from the survey method/conventional method of well-being measurement. Participatory well-being ranking along with its trajectory of upward-downward mobility addresses this concern and improves over conventional methods on the ground of the following points:

— Firstly, the condition of well-being/poverty are selected by the participants. In this case relevant reference can be found from Sen (1981) – "...the choice of 'conditions of deprivation' cannot be independent of 'feelings of deprivation'. Material objects cannot be evaluated in this context without reference to how people view them, and even if 'feelings' are not brought in explicitly, they must have an implicit role in the selection of 'attributes'),

— Secondly, the identification of relative deprivation is captured much extensively by the local people's knowledge, and

— Lastly, the conventional methods are not responsive enough to the changing feelings and conditions (criteria) of well-being varying with spatio-temporal variations.

Table 10.1 : Profile of upward-downward mobility in well-being status of Punglapur Village after LWS (I) intervention

Relative Well-Being	Well-Being Group	Name of the Family Head	Inprovement in the Project Period		Reasons for Improvement				Participated in the Projects activities							Exclusive Member of Village Organization
			Significant	To Some Extent	Rice	Nursery compost	Calf Rearing	Business	Improved Rice	Compost pit	Nursery	Calf Rearing	Bio Gas	Gramin Bank	Latrine	
1	2	3	4	5	6	7	8	9	10	11	12	13	14	15	16	17
1		Mamata Saha														
2		Bhabani Bagdi														
3	Group A	Kamal Bagdi		Y		Y	Y				Y	Y	Y		Y	2M
4	Destitute	Nakul Bagdi														
5		Satu Bagdi													Y	
6		Sunil Bagdi													Y	
7		Sisr Bagdi													Y	
8		Pari Bauri									Y	Y				
9	Group B	Dhulo Bagdi	Group A-Group B			Y						Y			Y	6M
10	Poorest	Bulo Bagdi	Group A-Group B			Y									Y	5F
11		Shanty Mallick													Y	
12		Sarat Bagdi	Group A-Group B												Y	
13		Dhananjay Bagdi													Y	
14		Bholanath Bagdi													Y	
15		Sukumar Bagdi	Group B-Group C		Y										Y	
16		Shankar Bagdi									Y				Y	
17		Promnila Saha									Y					

Continued.....

Table 10.1 *(Contd.)*

1	2	3	4	5	6	7	8	9	10	11	12	13	14	15	16	17
18		Dulal Bagdi												Y	Y	
19	Group C	Anil Bagdi													Y	5M
20	Poor	Madan Das													Y	6F
21		Jatan Bhagdi									Y					
22		Lakhindar Bagdi		Y		Y						Y			Y	
23		Dayanoy Saha	Group B-Group C					Y								
24		Madhusudan Bagdi									Y				Y	
25		Mantu Bagdi	Group B-Group C								Y				Y	
26		Fatik Saha		Y			Y									
27		Netai Bagdi	Group C-Group D		Y											
28	Group D	Bamacharan Saha	Group C-Group D					Y								2M
29		Manik Chandra Das		Y		Y						Y			Y	2F
30	Moderate	Bijoy Bagdi		Y		Y					Y	Y			Y	
31		Ashoke Bagdi		Y		Y					Y	Y				
32		Syama Chand Saha	Group C-Group E					Y								
33		Sahadev Das												Y	Y	
34		Lakhikanto Saha													Y	
35		Asim Bagdi	Group D-Group E		Y						Y	Y				

Continued......

Table 10.1: *(Contd.)*

1	2	3	4	5	6	7	8	9	10	11	12	13	14	15	16	17
36	Group E	Badan Saha														2M
37		Basudev Das	Group D-Group E								Y					1F
38	Well off	Dilip Saha			Y						Y	Y				
39		Bamacharan Chatterjee														
40		Madan Mohon Saha													Y	

Table 10.2 : Profile of upward-downward mobility in well-being Status at Kantamari after LWS (I) intervention

Well-being status of people	Number of family	Number of family whose status improved	Number of people who got LWS (I) assistance	Type of assistance from LWS (I)	Number of people whose economic status have not changed	Reasons for not chaning	Number of executive member in the village committee
1	2	3	4	5	6	7	8
GROUP A—Poorest	66	5	2	Rickshaw van shooting net for capturing fish spawns	61	Lack of capital Poor educational status rate of High rate of migration Alcoholism Lack of awareness on how to spend money	2
GROUP B—poor	120	21	13	Summer rice variety winter rice variety vegetable garden Rickshaw van	99	Lack of cooperation and linkage amongst one another Medical Expenses high family not planned alcoholism lack of capital	1
GROUP C—Moderate	88	60	47	Summer rice Winter rice Vegetable garden Chilli Paddy processing Pisciculture—(Rearing)	28	Lack of enough enthusiasm	8

Continued......

Table 10.2: *(Contd.)*

1	2	3	4	5	6	7	8
GROUP D— Better off	37	26	22	cum-stock pond and boat/net)Landshaping Grocery Poultry Summer rice Winter rice Vegetable garden Pisciculture (Rearing-cum-stock pond and boat/net) landshaping Poultry	11	Lack of enough enthusiasm	3

Table 10.3 : Profile of upward and downward mobility in well-being ladder in Dornakambala watershed after REACH interventions

Group	Families in 1997	Families in 2001	Families moving in downward direction	Families moving in upward direction	Reasons for no change in well-being ladder	Reasons for upward movement in well-being ladder (1-indicates direct effect due to watershed and 2 indicates indirect effect due to watershed)	Reasons for downward movement in well-being ladder
1	2	3	4	5	6	7	8
1. Well off	10	11		1		(i) Due to availability of sufficient water, cropping pattern changed and higher productivity was obtained.-1 (ii) Joined as a member in Haritha lakshmi group-2 (iii) Productivity is high in milch cattle & poultry birds-2	
2. Medium	20	22	1	4	Even though income comes there is no change in their position due to higher cost of living	(i). Additional income is obtaining from Dairy & Ghee prepatation-2 (ii) Profits obtained from mango orchards-1 (iii) Higher profitability from sericulture-1 (iv) Productivity of maize and sunflower has been increased-1	There is no earning male member in the families.

Continued.......

Table 10.3: *(Contd.)*

1	2	3	4	5	6	7	8
3. Poor	20	23	1	7		(i) high profitability from fish culturing in community pond-1 (ii) crop loans are obtained from financial institution like S.B.I-1 (iii) women joined as a member in S.H.G. like, Harithalakshmi groups etc.1	In few cases only some families incurring huge expenses for their daughters marriage hence it leads to declining movement.
4. Very poor	30	24				(i) proper utilization of agriculture labourers in most part of the year-2 (ii) profits obtained from poultry birds, goat & sheep -2	

Findings of the case studies

Case Study –1	Case Study –2	Case Study –3
Upward mobility is mostly due to the participation of the villagers in different agricultural and livestock interventions introduced by LWS for obtaining higher profits.	Improvement of the villagers is not the result of profits earned from agriculture and allied interventions only but also due to other income generating activities like van rickshaw pulling, grocery etc.	Farmers/villagers moved up ward in well-being ladder due to higher profits obtained from agriculture and livestock products.
In very few cases business is a key factor for upward mobility.	For poorest and poor group lack of capital, low educational status, alcoholism were major factors for their unimproved status. But for moderate and better off groups lack of enough enthusiasm was the reason for their un-changed position.	Farmers did not shown improvement in their living standard owing to large number of family members and high cost of living. Downward movement was been found mainly due to the absence of male earning members in the family.

Differences between the case studies

Case Study –1	Case Study –2	Case Study –3
1. Participants put destitute to well-off, these five groups in a descending manner on the basis of their perceptions. The mobility from, say, group A (destitute) to group B (poorest) empirically showed a downward mobility whereas it implied improvement or upward mobility.	Only those families, which improved their status were mentioned as it was not possible to mention all the names of heads of 311 families.	The participants arranged the groups from well off to very poor in a descending manner and thus interpretation became easier.
2. Intra group and inter-group mobility were also identified.	It was not clear whether the mobility was intra-group or inter-group.	Only inter-group mobility was shown.
3. It only showed the upward mobility and its reasons.	It showed the upward mobility with reasons and also the factors underlying situations, which remained unchanged.	It presented both upward and downward mobility with reasons behind them. It also examined the causes for non-change in the well-being of the farmers.

Conclusion

Well-being is a complex, diverse and dynamic reality having multiple local meaning and interpretation with capabilities and livelihoods as means, and equity and sustainability as principles. Hence, upward-downward mobility in well-being is rather a complex process as the people's idea of well-being changes rapidly with time. But "before-after" well-being ranking done by the participants makes this type of study easier and valid to a great extent as it is based on their local knowledge and experience, and need not to mention, the people at the receiving end can judge their conditions better.

It is quite evident that probing questions used in this method elicit the basic reasons underlying the upward-downward mobility or unchanged condition. These reasons are of paramount importance and demand further analysis. Until and unless they are scanned critically with both macro and micro perspectives, it is not possible to have broad based applications in the developmental processes and necessary modifications in the strategies of policy makers and programme planners.

REFERENCES

Chambers, R. (1990): *Rural Development: Putting the Last First.* Longman Scientific & Technical, Essex.

Chambers, R. (1997): *Whose Reality Counts? Putting First Last.* Intermediary Technology Publications, London.

Dasgupta, P. (1993): An Enquiry into Human Well-being and Destitution, Clarendon Press, Oxford.

Grandin, B. (1988): Wealth Ranking in Smallholder Communuties: a Field Manual, Intermediate Technology Publication, London.

Narayan, D., Patel, R. Schafft, K. Rademacher, A. and Koch-Schulte, S. (2000): *Voices of the Poor: Can Anyone Hear Us?* Oxford University Press, New York.

Sen, A. (1981): *Poverty and Famines, An Essay on Entitlement and Deprivation*, Oxford University Press, Oxford.

Sen, A. (1992): *Inequality Reexamined*, Oxford University Press, New Delhi.

Theis, J. and Grady, H.M. (1991): *Participatory Rapid Appraisal for Community Development: a Training Manual based on Experiences in the Middle-East and North Africa.* International Institute for Environment and Development and Save the Children Federation, London.

11

PARTICIPATORY AREA SELECTION FOR TECHNOLOGICAL INTERVENTION

RUPA DASGUPTA, SWATI LAHIRI, A.K. JHA and M.V.R.L. MURTHY

Introduction

Any measure with an aim to benefit the rural masses, be it technological or otherwise, meant for application/dissemination in the rural sector by an implementing agency in the first place should be need based [as identified by the local people] and preferably based on locally available resources. The rural masses should feel a sense of ownership as a part of the system intending to apply the technology either by monetary gains or through involvement and participation in any of the various activities involved in the implementation of the technology.

The present paper discusses a successful method that emerged during the implementation of an UNDP sponsored sub-programme on sustainable livelihoods through technology management packages. The paper focuses on the efforts made at selecting an appropriate technology, based on the resources available in the region through people's participation. The present paper discusses the process of selecting technologies from amongst the various available options and converting the technology into a technology management package (TMP) by linking it with the local people, resources, market and finance.

Thought behind the Study

One useful way of knowing the people's need and resource availability in the area is by conducting survey and a participatory resource mapping.

Usually sample surveys are undertaken for such purpose but it was felt for the present study that all household inclusive survey wouldbe more effective. This would help in knowing the people's mind and also help in forming a basis for judging individual preferences, capabilities and skills. Each member of the house was taken into consideration while conducting the survey for fulfilling the above purpose.

From the vast data generated, it is obvious that the needs identified were many. In the process of narrowing down the most essential and most sought after need was in terms of improving the quality of life of the rural people. The sub-programme under discussion also aimed at improving the quality of life of rural people mainly through technological inputs. For further progress in the programme it was thought that a village level meeting would help in narrowing down the most essential needs that would then constitute a community need arrived through consensus and the related technological areas, which would help in achieving the purpose, could then be identified. It was also decided that such meetings should be conducted by a social scientist who would be able to justify the choice of the community without hurting the sentiments of any individual or group of villagers.

Resource and Skill Identification

It was decided that under the sub-programme resource survey in addition to the household survey would also have to be conducted at the block and the village level for identifying local resource availability. This was considered essential as the technological inputs were mainly aimed at being local resource-based.

For village level resource mapping *patwari* maps were utilised. The resources of the villages were identified with the help of the villagers mainly during the village meeting or household survey when they were asked to identify the following in the village map:

- Cropland, pastureland, forestland, wasteland etc.;
- Mineral resources, forest resources;
- Animal husbandry/Livestock;
- Biomass;
- Crops and production;
- Rivers, canals, wells etc.;
- Other landmarks;
- Their own house; and
- Existing infrastructure facilities.

For Block level information, block profiles collected from respective block offices were utilised. The village resources identified by the villagers as a group were superimposed on the block map, to yield the local resource map. The block level resource maps included the following details:

- Village boundaries,
- Major roads,
- Telecommunication network,
- Banking facility,
- Market facility,
- Storage (cold)/Godowns,
- Industries, and
- Training Centre or Other Centres.

The skills available with the villagers could be of the following types:

- Traditional skills,
- Family skills, and
- Acquired skills through training or on jobs.

The skills would mainly relate to masonry, weaving, pottery, carpentry, handicraft, repair/maintenance of mechanical/electrical/electronic items, etc. Skill identification would serve to make a proper choice while selecting members for implementation of technologies. This list would emerge at the time of household survey and/or during village level meetings.

Technology Identification and Intervention

Any intervention under the present sub-programme had to be technology based. While thinking of any intervention, it was necessary to bear the following in mind:

(i) Choice of appropriate technology.
(ii) Ensuring synergy with local skills, materials and environment and disseminating demand driven technology to rural and urban poor.
(iii) Improving the quality of life, especially of women and under-privileged class of society through implementation of the sub-programme.
(iv) Helping in providing employment to the rural and urban poor thus affecting poverty alleviation, skill acquisition and/or up gradation and implementation of environmentally sound technologies for overall sustainable development.

While searching for appropriate technologies for dissemination to the rural masses, it was observed that there was no dearth of technologies or technology providers in the country. Rather the question arose as to why despite available resources and technologies there was hardly any match between the two? Why the rural sector, which was the bulk supplier of raw material and labour was unable to realize the benefits of the developed technologies? The answer was indicative—in terms of lack of concerted efforts in this direction. Hence, it was felt that instead of giving a technology as such there was a need for developing the technology into a complete package (TMP) with people's participation.

Keeping in mind the area of application of the TMP certain combination of characteristic features were thought to be important so that the technology package should be simple, stable, socially acceptable, sustainable and suitable with synergy between the technology aspect and its total management. The latter was in terms of both financial and marketing linkage, with consideration of its impact on society, environment, culture, economy and holistic aspects. The technology package would have to be demonstrated, applied, adopted and replicated at the unit/village level. For the above, the proposed technology package would require testing for its feasibility, followed by standardization and modification, if necessary, keeping in view the area of application. The details of the technology would have to be demonstrated and taught to group/s of people of the particular area who may form Self-Help Groups (SHG) for running such unit or enterprise.

Methodology

To realize the purpose and objective behind the present study, a few things were required to be arranged as follows:

- An implementing agency,
- Interest of the village people for whom the benefits were intended
- Availability of resource in the area,
- Choice of appropriate technology,
- Technology dissemination, and
- Market linkages.

In order to realize the programme objective, it is important to match all the above requirements. For this purpose, the role of the implementing agency, which could be a government organization or a non-government organization, was of utmost importance. They would have to ascertain the resource availability in the area and the need/interest of the people to utilize those resources for better use than the existing one. In case a particular resource was being gainfully utilized, it would be wise not to venture into further exploiting that resource. Resource availability in an area could be known from records or from discussion with the local people together with the quantity and quality of the resource and its existing use. Initially, to start with resource utilization should be restricted only to those, which were not fully utilized or not gainfully utilized. Later, depending on the success attained, the rest of the resource could also be used. Quality of the resource intended for use was also very important, as that would give an idea of the choice of technology. The interest of the local people to be associated with the TMP could be ascertained through survey or discussion. As the resources belonged to the local people, their willingness to experiment with their resource was also important. It was important for the local people to have a clear picture of the purpose and advantage of the TMP, and to understand the benefits that can accrue through their participation and support. It was important to explain that it is not an industry that was being set-up in their area, which would employ them.

Based on the quality and quantity of the resource available, technology was required to be chosen. The technology would generally add value to the resource. This could be done by either making it into a product or by processing the raw material/resource. Different technologies would be available and a proper choice was required based on the quality, quantity of the resource and also the cost, ease in availability and adaptability of the technology to the area.

For dissemination of the technology in the rural area, linkages were required to be established between the technology provider and the rural people who would implement the technology. In most cases, implementation of the technology would require a group of people and hence self-help groups (SHGs) could be formed and made functional as per normal practices. This meant that members of the SHG were required to meet regularly, open credit facilities amongst the members, open a bank account and generate self-financed resources. These criteria would prove useful for obtaining loans from banks or financial institutions, which would provide support for running the intended enterprise set-up by the technology.

Another important factor would be marketing of the product. This would somewhat depend on the quality and quantity of the produce. Any or more than one of the following methods could be adopted for marketing the product.

(i) *Links:* This could be established with known agencies, which market similar products and make products as per their specifications. This would require maintaining a strict vision on the quality of the produce.

(ii) *Marketing in nearby localities:* This could be done with setting up own brand name and registering for appropriate trade mark. This would depend on the quality of the produce for example food articles would require FPI or AGMARK certification. Non-food items in the above category could be given to dealers of similar product for supply to urban areas where there was a perceived demand for such items.

(iii) *Selling locally:* This would depend upon the demand of the produce/product locally. Non-food items or items frequently required for local consumption like organic compost, poultry products and nursery plants could be marketed at local outlets or through door-to-door selling.

(iv) *Marketing through dealers:* The products specially the non-food variety which does not require strict quality assurance like those mentioned in the above category could be given to dealers of similar product for supply to urban areas where there was a demand for such items.

Utility of the Study

Gainful utilization of raw material mainly lying unutilized or not getting proper value due to its poor quality or improper marketing was initially aimed at setting up enterprises through technological inputs wherein marketing of the material would also be taken care of. This would help in confidence building of the local people to gradually take up more challenging enterprises and extend the use of the raw material to other items.

Another utility of setting up proposed enterprises would be employment generation. This would help in income generation mainly through enterprise development and help restrict migration to greener pastures. Self-help groups would consist of both women and men members or some enterprises due to their nature could be completely women based ones; this would help maintain gender balance towards income of the family and help restrict atrocities on women common in rural India mainly due to the low economic status of women.

Setting up enterprises at their own level and successfully running them would help in building confidence of the villagers, specially as marketing would also be done by them. This would help them in realizing their own capabilities and restrict them in selling their own resources in the raw material form to middle men or for a low price.

Case Study

The implementing agency

The Centre for Advanced Research and Development (CARD) was the implementing agency. It was being implemented in the Ghughri block of Mandla district of Madhya Pradesh.

The resource

The Ghughri block of the Mandla district of Madhya Pradesh is a tribal block. It is rich in forest resources, amongst them rock honey is one abundantly available resource. This block has mainly rock bee honey, in which around 800 people work as honey hunters for additional income. Each honeycomb can yield around 3 to 15 kg of honey. The total quantity of honey would be substantial for setting up an enterprise for honey collection and processing, as could be understood from the present number of honey collectors and interest among the people for the profession, in spite of the low incomes generated.

The technology

Till the present intervention, honey was collected from trees by cumbersome techniques, which resulted in killing of bees causing ecological loss with very low yield of honey. The intervention proposed was honey extraction by scientific methods based on the technology of a known technology provider in the area. The technology involved use of water spray and protective dress to ensure the safety of the honey collector, a rope ladder to reach honey combs at inaccessible points/ heights and a clip for preserving the honey. In addition, bee wax and pollen were obtained after refining the honey. Their technology had the following advantages:

- Honeycomb or bees were not destroyed,
- Better quality honey could be collected,
- Yield could increase,
- Safety of honey collectors was addressed,
- Preserved the bee population by ensuring long lasting yield of honey,
- Multiplied the number of extractions from each colony of bees, and
- Provided higher income to honey collectors and processors.

After collection of the crude honey, it was transferred to a double walled stainless steel jacketed vessel provided with a heater at the bottom. The water in the outer jacket was slowly heated up to 60°C, which slowly provided heat to the honey in the inner vessel. This was done with an objective to lower the viscosity of the honey. The honey was then transferred for pressure filtration to a screw press; the process removed waxes and other extraneous matter. The filtered honey was stored in stainless steel containers.

SHGs

Self help groups of interested people were formed. Each group consisted of 8 to 10 persons, at least four of them were traditional honey hunters as this was a skill oriented job. Although there was a need for higher income generation and interest among the erstwhile honey collectors to join the SHGs, other people were not very interested. They had to be explained their role like they could engage in processing, packing and marketing to develop an interest. Many of the villagers agreed and joined the SHGs. Training was imparted to the SHG members in all aspects like honey collection, processing and packaging. A total of SHGs were operational during one season. The main season for honey collection was between November to March of a calendar year.

Financial Aspects of the Unit

The following costs/infrastructure were required for one unit of honey processing :

- Area for working (600 sq. feet)
- Cost of equipment
- Cost of raw material
- Processing cost
- Packaging
- Wages
- Cost of technology
- Marketing costs
- Preliminary and operative costs
- Fixed investments other than equipments
- Working capital
- Utility expenses

Calculating in the above manner the total working capital for one complete season would be around Rs., 1,70,000, which could be broadly calculated as in table on next page.

S.No.	Particular	Cost per season
1	Raw material	1,00,000
2	Packaging	30,000
3	Utility	3,000
4	Wages	20,000
5	Miscellaneous	5,000
6	Fixed investment including equipment	50,000
	Total	2,08,000

The money could be obtained by SHGs through bank or loans from financial institutions. Some of the costs were a one-time investment and some were recurring expenses. Costing of unit price could be done accordingly.

Marketing: Due to non-availability of quality honey in the local market and from unrecognized vendors people generally opted for standard manufacturers. Since this was a food item FPO or AGMARK certification was necessary. The output from the present enterprise was linked to the product manufactured and marketed by a local yet reputed manufacturer.

Potential areas where such enterprises can be replicated

This new enterprise could be replicated in areas having the following:

- The area should have a large bee population, which would normally co-exist with large forested areas, hilly tracks and several water bodies.
- Varied blooming vegetation in the area would be preferred since this would lead to better quality and higher quantity of honey.
- Existing groups and practices of honey collection in the area should exist, since this would ensure familiarity with hive location, wild bee behaviour and provide a skill base for partners in the SHGs.
- Availability of government funds is required for the initiative.

Concluding Remarks

Attaining self-sustainability is a common dream of both an individual and of the nation. Keeping in mind the vast resource of India, its diversity in terms of manpower availability coupled with the high standards of technology, many TMPs can be identified and made functional through people's participation. The above discussion sets up a modality wherein the available technology in the country is matched with the resources available with the rural masses; forming of enterprises through synchronization of the above two, with an aim to generate employment and income opportunities in the rural areas.

Acknowledgements

The contents of the paper is an outcome of the exercise done during implementation of an UNDP-DST-GOI supported programme on "Support to Rural Technology Development and Application Centres and block level Technology Resource Centres". This programme is being implemented at the Regional Research Laboratory, Bhopal that is a constituent R&D laboratory under the Council of Scientific & Industrial Research (C.S.I.R.). The authors are thankful to the sponsor of the sub-programme for providing an opportunity to be associated with such a sub-programme.

12

INNOVATIONS FROM THE FIELD
The Ownership/Empowerment Chappati

NEELA MUKHERJEE, SHAISTA KHAN and REKHA BAHUGUNA

PRA methods are never static. They are flexible, innovative and adaptive to local situation. Their strength lies in ways that they can be moulded to suit local context, circumstances and issues. This note describes some innovations in doing Chappati diagramming. In recent years there has taken place innovation and adaptation in Chappati/institutional diagramming at the field level so as to tailor them to measure "ownership", "empowerment", "decision-making", "involvement", "relationship", "accountability", "participation" and other social aspects of institutional development. Such adaptations have taken place in the field during participatory sessions related to impact assessment/participatory evaluation of rural institutions in different projects.

'Chappati' (Venn) Institutional Diagramming

Chappati/Venn diagrams are useful in the study of relationships of institutions/individuals with local communities. Venn/Chappati/ Institutional diagramming is a "visual" method to represent the role of individuals/institutions and their importance in decision-making. In such diagrams circle/s of different size represent individual/s and/or institution/s, whose size shows its degree of importance in local decision-making and the overlapping of circles indicate overlapping in decision-making. Overlapping of circles could arise due to one institution/individual interacting with another institution/individual in which case the circles overlap on one another. Such overlaps may be large or small depending on the extent of such interaction. If the circles are separate, then the institutions have no contact and if they touch upon each other there is information passing between institutions. Strong/weak linkages between two institutions represented by two circles can also be shown by steady/ broken lines/arrows.

"Ownership/ Empowerment" Chappati

A variation of the usual Venn/Chappati diagram termed as Ownership/ Empowerment Chappati *(depending on the aspect under discussion whether "ownership", "empowerment" or some other criteria)* was applied to different villages for studying relationships within members of local institutions such as self-help groups, user-groups and other village-based institutions. In such Ownership/Empowerment Chappati the villagers construct their Chappati (a single Venn diagram, see Chart 12.1) on ownership/empowerment of each individual and identify the individual's socio-economic group based on indigenous criteria. As a "visual" output the advantage is that with proper facilitation, the control of the interactive process can be with the local group members who are involved in constructing the Empowerment/Ownership Chappati diagram. It is best to use different labels in the Chappati, depending on whether "ownership" or "empowerment" is being analysed.

Construction of Ownership Chappati

In one village, for example, this method was applied for learning about "ownership" aspects of members within the SHG. For this purpose, a big size chart paper was taken and the members of local women's SHG helped each other to draw a circle (or Ownership Chappati) with the aid of a round-shape "thali" (metal plate). The centre-point of the circle represented the highest degree of "ownership" and points away from it showed lower degrees of the same. The names of the members of SHG were written on small chits of paper and discussed in terms of individual feeling of ownership of such local institution. Based on such discussion the names of the members were then placed near the centre point or away from it depending on the degree of "ownership" shown by each member. For informing the Ownership Chappati the socio-economic status of households (whether poor, medium or rich) was also indicated against the names of the members with the help of symbols. This helped in self-assessment of "ownership" of different social strata in the village and also in terms of furthering project objective of involving poor people in that locality.

What the Ownership Chappati showed?

Some related points depicted by the Ownership Chappati are indicated below:

(i) The degree of institutional ownership by its members and high/ low ownership and the criteria for determining such ownership.
(ii) Those who participated and benefited from institutions and the extent of their participation and benefit.
(iii) The sense of responsibility and the degree of accountability of individuals towards institutions and the extent of participation in decision-making.
(iv) The degree of empowerment accompanying the process of ownership, which has taken place through the institution in question.
(v) Names of those individual/s empowered and still to be empowered/not empowered.

Chart 12.1: Empowerment/Ownership Chappati

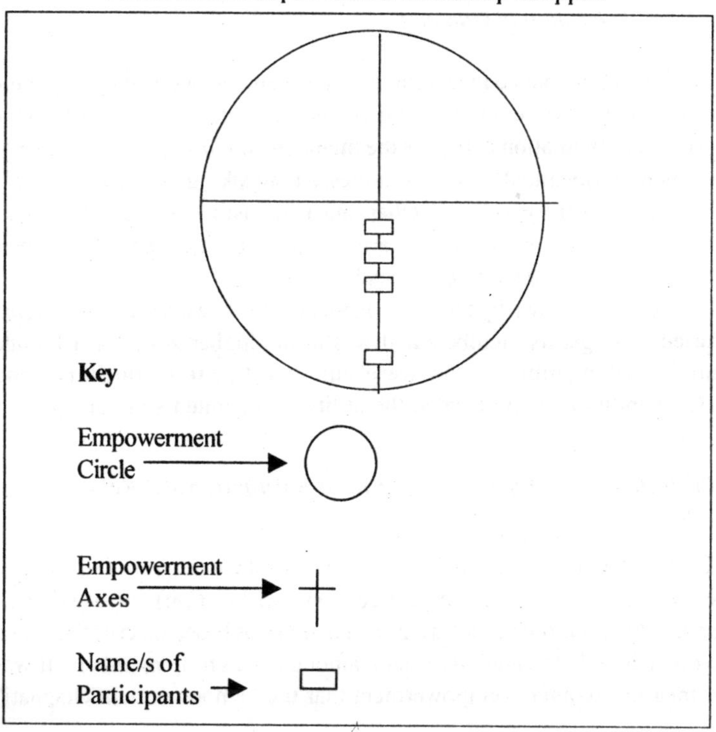

Illustrations from the Field: Village Siriyo, Rishikesh, Uttaranchal, India

"Ownership" Chappati of Village-level Organization

One issue explored is about the sense of ownership of village level organization called *Garema (Village-based community organization facilitated by the project)* by its members. Whether the members owned *Garema* and its activities and if so to what extent. The members considered four aspects for constructing such an Ownership Chappati (a circular space) for *Garema* in which names of all members were ranked as per the criteria. These aspects were in terms of four axes of that Empowerment Chappati (a circular space), namely,

- Attendance in meeting,
- Plantation,
- Taking Responsibility, and
- Awareness level about role of village-level federation called *Corema (inter-village-based organization representing federation of Garema).*

About attendance in meetings only 3 members were attending them most regularly while some other members had better attendance than the rest. About plantation activities the members of *Garema* were ranked as per their involvement in such activities. About taking responsibility only 4 members were good at discharging responsibility about *Garema's* activities. Regarding level of awareness about *Corema* only 4 members were aware and took interest in such activities.

Hence, as shown by the above indicators the "ownership" of *Garema* varied amongst its members and was in the higher zone for a limited number of members, who were enthusiastic, took initiative and responsibility and appreciated the utility of federated structure such as *Corema.*

Illustration from Field: Village Kheda Rasulpur, Kota, Rajasthan, India

This was group-evaluation done by members of women self-help groups, (each exercise done in separate session and location) for a women's empowerment project. The group-evaluation was based on criteria, which evolved locally through discussion amongst the group members. It was to measure women's empowerment that the "empowerment chappati" was applied by the members and the information generated was found useful as lesson learnt in the course of the end-of-the project evaluation carried out by the members themselves. The women found the method empowering in the sense that they could evolve their own criteria based on project objectives and then evaluate them in terms of what they thought was empowering and the degree of such empowerment of each member.

At first, the members listed the objectives of the Mahila Mandal (Self-Help Group/SHG of women) and then they together did the Empowerment Chappati based on such objectives. Three Empowerment Chappati's constructed separately by the three self-help groups of women showed how individual members of the three groups performed in their own groups. It had 4 axes on which women group assessed 4 aspects of SHG from the central point of the Empowerment Chappati. The 4 aspects were as follows:

- Number of persons they motivated for literacy,
- Number of persons motivated for family planning,
- Their income from tailoring skills acquired through project activities, and
- Increase in courage and confidence, on an individual basis.

Empowerment as measured by SHG members included their achievement in terms of providing motivation for literacy and that for family planning. They thought that the SHG movement had enabled them to reduce female illiteracy in that locality and also helped in empowering other women (non-members) in terms having small families. Both indicators showed contribution towards women's progress by SHG members.

The three charts showing empowerment of individual members of different SHGs of women portray an overall picture as shown in Table 12.1 Summary results are indicated below.

Table 12.1: Overall Picture of Empowerment of Women Self-Help Groups

Names of Members	Number motivated for literacy	Number motivated for family planning	Income generation (in Indian Rupees)	Increase in confidence and courage (Number)
Total for Mahila Mandal 1— "Rajlakhsmi Sahayta Samuh"	265	355	83,000	High—3 Medium—2 Low—7
Total for Mahila Mandal 2— "Anand Sahayta Samuh"	111	458	2,60,000	High—3 Medium—3 Low—5
Total for Mahila Mandal 3— "Bajrang Sahayta Samuh"	235	348	1,57,000	High—3 Medium—1 Low—7
Total	611	1161	5,00,000	High—9 Medium—6 Low—19

- Table 12.1 shows wide variations in terms of empowerment of individual members of self-help groups across the three groups. The chart shows that the members of self-help groups 1 and 3 had performed better in motivating others for literacy classes while those in 2 had motivated higher number of individuals for family planning practices. In terms of generating income from skills acquired through project, group 2 had performed better while members of group 3 had a slight edge with regard to increase in courage and confidence as compared to other groups.
- In terms of numbers, those motivated for family planning seems to be higher than those motivated to join literacy class, which is clearly pronounced in all the three self-help groups. One plausible reason was that there were not many individuals to be motivated for joining literacy classes since in that village the literacy rate was relatively high.
- In terms of income generation through skill building (e.g. sewing and tailoring skills) the range of financial empowerment was between Rs. 60,000 to none. Skill building helped in sourcing of livelihood for many women and led to income generation.
- There were positive changes in courage and confidence of most women members though the change in position of individual members as placed in the Empowerment Chappati or Venn diagram showed wide variations. For a few members such positive change was high with a major increase in courage and confidence, while for some it was on a medium range and for many others such change was on the lower side.

Some Lessons Learnt

(i) The concept of using the symbol of "Chappati" was dear to the heart of women. They prepared Chappati on a daily basis and served their family members as food. Men ate them hence felt close to the Chappati.

(ii) Placement/Ranking by members required proper group discussion to be free of bias to the extent possible.

(iii) There was a process of 'warming up' before the exercise was done. This generally involved discussion of objectives and activities of the institution/s under reference.

(iv) Listing and then ranking/grouping of institutions in terms of their significance/relevance helped in easy construction of Empowerment Chappati by groups.

(v) Empowerment Chappati followed by analysis of criteria and possible action/s were generally more effective.

(vi) Well-being grouping after construction of Empowerment Chappati provided insights into the issue of "whose empowerment/ownership?" and "how much?"

Limitations

Some limitations of the method were as follows:

- In case of institutions with large number of members such diagramming could become a time consuming exercise.
- Much discussion was required for placement of the names of members on the Empowerment/Ownership Chappati and conflicts tend to arise, which need to be resolved amicably.
- Placement of names on the Empowerment Chappati became easier when considerable discussions took place amongst the participants.

INDEX